The War We Wage

TAYLOR KERBY

WESTBOW°
PRESS
A DIVISION OF THOMAS NELSON
& ZONDERVAN

WestBow Press books may be ordered through
booksellers or by contacting:

WestBow Press
A Division of Thomas Nelson & Zondervan
1663 Liberty Drive
Bloomington, IN 47403
www.westbowpress.com
1 (866) 928-1240

ISBN: 978-1-4908-7122-6 (sc)

Library of Congress Control Number: 2015903195

Print information available on the last page.

WestBow Press rev. date: 3/31/2015

CONTENTS

PREFACE

Wake Up to the War

Are you awake? Seriously, are you awake? I am not asking if your eyes are open or if you are out of your bed. It does not matter how long you have been out of your room today either. None of that determines whether you are awake or not. The definition of being awake is to become cognizant. This means that if you are truly awake then you are aware. Are you aware of everything happening around you? Most people are not fully aware of everything happening around them. Some know but try to act like there is nothing and live in their own little world. Then there are the rare few that know exactly what is happening around them and are fighting. We need to be awake to the war around us. No matter who you are or what you believe, there is a war for your life going on right now. It is a war that began before you were even born. It began before your grandparents were born. It began at the first sin ever committed. That is when the war started and it will never end until the renewal of all creation. It is hard to believe that there is this war because it is invisible. It is in the unseen realm. It is supernatural. That is also why it is the most dangerous war there has ever been and ever will be. Because it is unseen, we are rarely awake to it and are not always able to defend ourselves from the attacks that come our way. The worst part is that Christians are not awake to it and they are the people that need to be fighting the most. So how do we wake up to what is not seen? The war itself is not seen but the effects are seen every day and they are screaming at us to wake up. Someone lies to you and says that you are useless. Wake up! Someone steals a television. Wake up! Someone commits suicide. Wake up! Someone murders another person. Wake up! Brother kills his own brother. Wake up! Son kills his own parents. Wake up! Teenagers shoot other teens at their school. Wake up! College students massacre other students and professors at their college. Wake up! Someone plants a bomb that kills thousands. Wake up! There is a genocide that kills millions. Wake up! There is a war that kills countless amounts of innocent people. Wake up! There is an attempted extermination of an entire race of people. Wake up! Are you awake to the war? This stuff happens every day and people sleep right through it. The only time people seem to actually wake up is when it happens to them, but at that time it is already too late. We cannot wait for tragedy to strike before we begin to stand and fight. Wake up! Wake up! Wake up!

CHAPTER 1

Starting to Fight

Every person in the world is a part of the greatest and longest war in history. This war is the Spiritual War. Most people do not believe in this battle because of the word "spiritual". This means that it is not seen and that is has to do with a greater power than just humans. This is a battle between the God of the universe, the ultimate power over all, and the devil. People do not believe in this war because of their unbelief in God. Even some Christians choose not to believe in this war because it puts great pressure on them to be warriors in the spirit realm. We can try to ignore this war the best we can, but that does not mean it is not real. I understand why we would want to ignore this war. This war is hard. We are dealing with things that we cannot see and because of that it is extremely hard to defend ourselves from the blows that will come our way. This is like boxing while having a blindfold on. The only way to know when we are attacked is by knowing God and having Him lead you. This is also a scary war because we are dealing with other powers than just with machine guns and bombs. We are dealing with the powers of the spirit realm which includes demons. We are dealing with things that we do not fully understand and that makes us terrified of this war. We also ignore the war because if we realize that we are in a war, then it means that there is good and evil. We do not want to believe that anything is evil because we love looking at the world as being completely perfect where there is nothing ever wrong and that everything we do is good. If there is evil, then this world is broken and cannot be fixed by humans otherwise it would be perfect already. Evil will also mean that some of the actions we do are bad and not good. We want to believe that if we tell a little white lie that it is fine; if we steal small things it is okay; if we have sex with many people, everything will be fine in the end. We want to believe that it is fine to be a homosexual. We want to believe that an abortion is actually a moral way to deal with something that will cause hardship in life. We want to believe that people are basically good when they are truly basically evil. This keeps us from realizing or waking up to the war. I understand why we do not want to believe that all this is wrong and that there is a war, but if we ignore it then we have already lost. Just knowing that we are in a war is a great part of the victory.

Spiritual Warfare is not some event. It is not a time that we get together with other Christians and rebuke the devil in prayer. That is acute spiritual warfare. Spiritual Warfare is always happening. It is in what we think about, what we watch, what we say, what we do, and even our interactions with others. Spiritual Warfare is all around us and never stops. We are always being faced with it. We sometimes assume that it is over because we overcame a temptation to do something evil, but that is just a mere victory over a small battle. This war is still happening and just when you think you have won is usually the time that you will be attacked the greatest.

The greatest place that spiritual warfare is addressed is of course the Bible. 2 Corinthians 10:3 says that we do not war according to the flesh. Verse 4 then says that the weapons of warfare are not carnal. This means that this war is not physical and that we do not fight in it with ordinary weapons. 1 Peter 2:11 says that we need to abstain from fleshly lusts which wage war against our soul. This means that the things of our flesh, our physical wants and desires, are fighting against our soul, which is our eternal being and is what defines good and evil. The flesh is always seeking it own desires and never doing the things that God desires. The flesh is prideful, jealous, envious, hateful, and will lead us astray every time. We cannot follow our flesh and have victory in the war. 2 Timothy 2:3 says that we must endure hardship as being a soldier of Jesus Christ. This means that when we engage in spiritual warfare there will be many hardships because we are a soldier of Jesus Christ. There are many other verses in the Bible that address Spiritual Warfare, these are just a couple. Now I want to quote the most famous passage about Spiritual Warfare. This is the passage that will be used throughout this book to teach how to fight in this war. The passage is Ephesians 6:10-17. "Finally, my brethren, be strong in the Lord and in the power of His might. Put on the whole armor of God that you may be able to stand against the wiles of the devil. For we do not wrestle against flesh and blood, but against principalities, against powers, against the rulers of darkness of this age, against spiritual hosts of darkness in heavenly places. Therefore take up the whole armor of God that you may be able to withstand in the evil day, and having done all, to stand. Stand therefore, having girded your waist with truth, having put on the breastplate of righteousness, having shod your feet with the preparation of the gospel of peace; above all taking the shield of faith with which you will be able to quench all the fiery darts of the wicked one. And take the helmet of salvation and the sword of the Spirit, which is the Word of God." This is the most famous passage of Scripture about Spiritual Warfare and describes everything that we need to be effective in the fight. For now we will just look at verse 10 of Ephesians 6. Verse 10 says, "Finally be strong in the Lord." By using the word finally it means that there have been things already said that lead up to being strong in the Lord. The book of Ephesians is a letter to the church in Ephesus written by Paul addressing two major things. The first is to know who you are in Christ. We must first know who we are in Christ before we are able to engage effectively in Spiritual warfare. We must know who Christ has made us and how His death on the cross has affected us. First, by Christ dying on the cross He has made us pure and blameless. We are forgiven because Christ suffered and died for our sin. We must understand that we are no longer tainted by sin and that God does not see any sin that we have done or will ever do if we have surrendered our life to Christ. The only way to be forgiven by sin is to give our life over to Christ and have Him lead our life. We then need to understand that if God sees no sin in us then the devil cannot accuse us anymore. The devil will always try to disqualify us from fighting this war by showing you your sin. If we start to believe that we have sinned too much to have God's love, then we will submit to the devil and the war is already lost and you will go to Hell. We cannot listen to the lies of the enemy but must combat them with the truth that we are forgiven from all our sins by Jesus' death on the cross. The second thing that Paul addresses in Ephesians is living responsibly for God on a regular basis. It is not enough for us to surrender to Christ and then just go on sinning. We need to live responsibly for God by trying our hardest not to sin. We will still sin, but if we are truly repentant in our heart when we sin, then God is still forgiving toward us. It is when we continue sinning and using Christ's death as a license that we don't have to pay for it that make us not able to be forgiven by God. We must understand that we will sin but that when we do we can run to Jesus and ask for His forgiveness and then continue on trying not to fall back into sin. These two things are extremely important if we are to fight in this war. If you have not ever given your life to Christ and want to surrender your life to Him, I want you to right now just pray to Him and ask Him to forgive you and allow Him to become the ruler of your heart. I do not want you to do this just so that you can fight in Spiritual Warfare but I do want you to know the love and saving grace of Jesus. If you have prayed to God and asked Him to forgive you and have given your life over to Christ then you are truly forgiven and the devil cannot accuse you of your sin anymore. You are washed clean and blameless and the stain of sin is no longer on you. By knowing this we are now able to stand strong in the Lord as Ephesians 6:10 says. Now being in the Lord is a state of being. If you are in the Lord then you are strong. If you are not in the Lord then you are not strong. It is a state of being which means that we absolutely choose to be in the Lord. Paul was saying that in light of whom we are in Christ we are able to choose to be in the Lord and by that we are able to live responsibly. This all leads to how we are to fight in Spiritual Warfare.

Later in Ephesians 6:11 it says that we do not wrestle against flesh and blood. This means that it is first of all not against people. This is another reason why it is a hard battle to fight because we are all fighters by nature. We all have an inherent desire to see justice served. If you don't believe me then just look at all the television shows that have to do with the law and investigation. There are three Law and Order series, three CSI series, three NCIS series, and two Criminal Minds series. These are just the most well known ones. We love to see justice come and when we don't, we become angry and will fight for the person to pay. If justice is not paid, our back up emotion is to fight because God has put this desire into us so that we will fight this war. This is shown in movies like Gladiator and A Time to Kill. In both of these movies a person does a horrendous evil and gets away with it or is most likely to get away with it. Because of that certain people go and make them pay for what they have done. They become fighters. In Spiritual Warfare justice will not be paid until Christ comes back. Because we do not see justice be paid, we automatically want to fight back. The problem is that if we do not fight the devil then we are fighting people. The second thing we must learn from verse 11 is that it is supernatural. This means that if we don't fight the devil and fight people we are having a negative effect in the Spirit world. We are called by Christ to love everyone, even our enemies. If we do not love, then anything we do in the Spirit world would be of no use. In 1 Corinthian 13:1 Paul says, "If I speak in the tongues of men and angels, but have not love, I am only a clanging gong or a resounding cymbal." We must have love otherwise anything we do is useless. Before ever starting to fight in this war we must understand that there is a war, be strong in the Lord, and make sure that when we fight we are fighting the right enemy.

Lastly, to start fighting we must know that the devil has strategies. All the good and evil in the world comes from personalities. All good comes from God. All evil comes from personalities that are demonic and human. This is what the devil uses. The devil has fallen angels who are demons and they fight on his side. He is also able to use other humans to make us stumble. The demons are the ones that tempt us with evil desires and they will try to use humans to push the temptation. For example, the demon will say that we should be jealous or envious of a certain person. These are both bad feelings and can lead us to do terrible things. Demons can also use immodestly dressed women to have men lust after and it will lead them to all kinds of sexual impurity. These are the most well-known strategies of the devil. Spiritual Warfare is learning to recognize the strategies, refusing to cooperate, and cutting it off in Jesus' name. Every strategy of the devil leads to deception, bondage, and destruction. Jesus is the only one that can break these off. Sadly, many people do not go to Jesus first. In fact, people will use divination, horoscopes, and palm readers for help and these are strategies used by the devil as well. We only need Jesus and He is the only one that can help us have victory in this war. There are two major ways to recognize the strategies that the devil will use against you. The first is to ask yourself that if you were the devil, what would I do to myself. For instance, if a man knows that he has had a past with pornography, he knows that this is still a daily struggle for him and that it is very easy to fall back into. By knowing this he is able to know that the devil will most likely use lustful thought to make him fall back into pornography. This can even be the same case for some women. We need to know how we are attacked so that we can defend ourselves. When we know this, we need to then use Jesus to cut it off. Any time the temptation comes our way we can pray to Jesus and just tell Him that we are being tempted and ask Him to make the devil flee in His name. At the name of Jesus the devil must flee because Jesus is so much more powerful and will frankly kick the devil's butt. We also need to have people that we are accountable to that we can call at any time and ask them to pray with us to not fall into temptations. Then if we do fall, we need them to pray with us for forgiveness and the strength to turn away from that sin when it rears its ugly head again. The last way to shut down the devil is knowing Scripture. Luke 4:1-13 tells the story of when Jesus was in the wilderness and the devil came and tempted Him. Every time the devil tempted Him Jesus would answer with Scripture from the book of Deuteronomy and would not fall into sin. It then says in Ephesians

6:13 that the devil departed until a more opportune time. We need to know Scriptures that we can pull out to use against the devil, but also understand that even when we overcome him, he will be back to tempt us again. For example Ephesians 5:16 says, "But among you there must not be even a hint of sexual immorality." I have used this verse to overcome temptations when I want to lust after a woman. I just quote it and then command the devil to leave in Jesus' name. One thing to also notice about when Jesus answers the devil is that He never said the specific verse. He always answered saying, "It is written." We do not absolutely need to know exactly where the verse is located, (even though that is a good thing), but we just need to know what it says and we can use it against the devil.

The second way to help recognize strategies that the devil will use against you is to simply ask God. If we ask God to help us fight against the devil, He will give us everything we need and will tell us what to do to defend ourselves from the attacks. Now you are ready to at least start fighting in this war. The rest of this book will go into more detail about who our enemy is, angels and demons, and the armor of God. This will all help us to become expert soldiers for Christ in Spiritual Warfare. One more thing to consider is that the Ephesus came from an occult background that was deep in divination and workings of the devil. This is why Paul wrote so heavily about Spiritual Warfare and gave them every piece of armor they needed. We have the armor now need to put it on.

CHAPTER 2

Knowing Your Enemy

Sun Tzu wrote in his book <u>The Art of War</u>, "Therefore, I say: Know your enemy and know yourself; in a hundred battles, you will never be defeated." This is the most important rule of warfare. Know your enemy. In the last chapter I talked about how we must know who we are in Christ and that we are washed clean of sin and that God does not see sin in us anymore. That has to do with knowing yourself. Now we need to discuss knowing our enemy. Everyone should know that our enemy is the devil but that is not what knowing our enemy means. Knowing the enemy is truly knowing who the enemy is, why they are against you, and in what ways do they attack. In this chapter we are going to look at who he truly is.

Ephesians 6:11 says, "Put on the whole armor of God, that you may be able to stand against the schemes of the devil." In this war we are fighting to stand against the schemes of the devil. He is the true enemy. In Genesis 3 the enemy is introduced as the serpent. This means that the devil portrayed himself as a snake to deceive Eve so that she would disobey God and that her husband, Adam, would follow. In Revelation 12:3 he is shown as a fiery dragon with seven heads and ten horns with seven crowns on his head. So which one of these verses depicts who the enemy truly is? The truth is that all of these depict the enemy perfectly. The devil is able to portray himself in many different ways and these are two ways in which the Bible shows him being portrayed. As I said before in Genesis 3, he is referred to as a serpent. When using serpent as a noun it means a snake but if used as a verb it means to practice divination. This is what the devil does. He practices divination of Himself and deceives us to do it too. Revelation 12:9 says, "So the great dragon was cast out, that serpent of old, called the Devil and Satan, who deceives the whole world; he was cast to the earth, and his angels were cast out with him." The devil is the great dragon and the serpent. This verse also says that he was cast to the earth with his angels. To understand what that means we need to look at what happened with him and who he was before he was cast to the earth.

The beginning of Ephesians 6:12 says, "For we do not wrestle against flesh and blood, but against principalities." Principality comes from the Greek word Arche which means beginning, origins, the first person in a series, and top ruler. This means that we wrestle against something that has been around for a very long time. We also wrestle against something that understands authority because it had authority and still does. In the beginning, Satan was not a serpent. He was a servant. In the beginning there were three archangels and each one had authority over angels. The archangels were created to serve God. The first archangel was Gabriel. His name meant God is my strength. In Daniel 8:16 it says, "And I heard a man's voice between the banks of Ulai, who called, and said, "Gabriel, make this man understand the vision." Later in Daniel 9:21 Daniel is speaking and he says, "Yes, while I was speaking in prayer, the man Gabriel, whom I had seen in a vision at the beginning, being caused to fly swiftly, reached me about the time of the evening offering." In the New Testament when Zacharias was told that he would have a son that would later become John the Baptist Luke 1:19 says, "And the angel answered and said to him, "I am Gabriel, who stands in the presence of God, and was sent to speak to you and bring these glad tidings." Then a few verses later in Luke 1:26 it says, "Now in the sixth month the angel Gabriel was sent by God to a city of Galilee named Nazareth." This is when Gabriel went to Mary and told her that she would conceive and give birth to Jesus. Gabriel is the messenger of God. He was the archangel that would be sent to bring messages to people. He was sent to declare the birth of John the Baptist and Jesus as shown by the verses just listed. He also met with Daniel about a vision. His job in heaven was to bring messages from God to people on earth. The second archangel was named Michael, which means who is like God. In Daniel 10:13 it says, "But the prince of the kingdom of Persia withstood me twenty-one days; and behold, Michael, one of the chief princes, came to help me, for I had been left alone there with the kings of Persia." Later in the same chapter, verse 21 says, "But I tell you what is noted in the Scripture of Truth. "No one upholds me against these, except Michael your prince." Then the first half of Daniel 12:1 says, "At that time Michael shall stand up, the great prince who stands watch over the sons of your people." He is also mentioned in the New Testament. Jude 1:9 says, "Yet Michael the archangel, in contending with the devil, when he disputed about the body of Moses, dared not bring against him a reviling accusation but said, "The Lord rebuke you!" Then the last verse is Revelation 12:7 which says, "And war broke out in heaven: Michael and his angels fought with the dragon; and the dragon and his angels fought." This verse also proves that archangels are leaders over the other angels because it says that Michael and his angels fought. He had angels under him that were following him into this battle. Michael is the commander and leader of the armies of God. He is the one that went to fight against the dragon and he also contended with the devil as shown in the verses above. His job was to lead the armies of God into battle against the devil and those that are against Him. The last archangel's name is Heylel. His name means Light Bearer or to reflect, to carry, or to wear. Isaiah 14:12 says, "How you have fallen from heaven, O Lucifer, son of the morning! How you are cut down to the ground, You who weakened the nations!" The name Heylel translated into English is Lucifer. This is the archangel that is also known as the devil and Satan. Satan was once one of the most important principalities in heaven. Satan was not always a serpent. At the beginning he was a servant. He was an archangel of God but rebelled and was cast out of heaven. Now that we know this we need to find out how he became our enemy.

Ezekiel 28 is a passage of Scripture that was written to the King of Tyre. Some portions of this chapter are addressing the man, while other portions are addressing the spirit behind the man, which is Satan. Ezekiel 28:11-18 says, "Moreover the word of the Lord came to me, saying, "Son of man, take up a lamentation for the King of Tyre, and say to him, Thus says the Lord God: You were the seal of perfection, full of wisdom and perfect in beauty. You were in Eden, the garden of God; every precious stone was your covering: The sardius, topaz, and diamond, Beryl, onyx, and jasper, Sapphire, turquoise, and emerald with gold. The workmanship of your timbrels and pipes was prepared for you on the day you were created. You were the anointed cherub who covers; I established you; you were on the holy mountain of God; you walked back and forth in the midst of fiery stones. You were perfect in your ways from the day you were created, till iniquity was found in you. By the abundance of your trading you became filled with violence within, and you sinned; therefore I cast you as a profane thing out of the mountain of God; and I destroyed you, O covering cherub, from the midst of the fiery stones. Your heart was lifted up because of your beauty; you corrupted your wisdom for the sake of your splendor; I cast you to the ground, I laid you before kings that they might gaze at you. You defiled your sanctuaries by the multitude of your iniquities, by the iniquity of your trading; therefore I brought fire from your midst; it devoured you, and I turned you to

ashes upon the earth in the sight of all who saw you."
This passage was not addressing the King of Tyre but
was addressing Satan because he was the spirit that
was behind the King. Now I want to walk through this
entire passage to see what God is saying about Satan.
In verse 12 it says that Satan had the seal of perfection.
Satan was created and designed by God. Satan was not
created evil. It then says that he was in Eden, which
shows he is not talking to the King of Tyre because
he was not ever in Eden. It says that Satan had nine
precious stones for his covering. The word for covering
in Hebrew means decoration, adornment, and armor. It
then says that he had timbrels and pipes. Isaiah 14:11
says talking about Satan, "Your pomp is brought down
to Sheol, and the sound of your stringed instruments;
the maggot is spread under you, and worms cover you."
This verse says that he had stringed instruments as
well. The timbrel was for percussion. The pipes were
for woodwinds. The stringed instrument was a harp.
These were actually all built into Satan. It then says at
the end of verse 14 that he walked in the midst of the
stones of fire. The stones of fire mean the presence of
God. Satan used to be in the presence of God when he
was in heaven. Verse 15 says that he was blameless until
iniquity was found in him. He was perfect in everything
but then iniquity was found in him because he became

prideful. His name was Heylel which means light bearer, which comes from the Hebrew word halel which means to boast. Satan's job in heaven was to boast of God. He was heavens worship leader. He ushered all the glory and worship to God. He was also the instrument that God would breathe through to make music for Himself. The stones that Satan was covered with were stones that would reflect the Shekinah Glory of God. Shekinah means the entire and fullness of His glory. Satan saw the fullness of God's glory and was created to boast about it. So why was Satan fired? Verse 18 says that it was by the iniquity of his trading. His trade was to usher all worship and glory to God. Satan actually began to keep some of the worship for himself instead of ushering all the worship to God. He became prideful and wanted to be exalted like God. Isaiah 14:13 says talking about Satan, "For you have said in your heart: I will ascend into heaven, I will exalt my throne above the stars of God; I will also sit on the mount of the congregation and the farthest sides of the north; I will ascend above the heights of the clouds, I will be like the Most High." He wanted to be just like God. Notice that he did not want to be higher than God. He was in the presence of God and saw the entire fullness of His glory. Satan knows that there is no way anything could be higher than God but he wants to be like God. Because of this he was cast out of heaven and it says that a third of the angels were cast out with him. There were three archangels that each had charge over other angels which would mean that they each had charge over a third of the angels. Satan was able to deceive the angels that were under him to give him glory because they were also created to worship God as Satan was. Revelation 12:4 says, "His tail drew a third of the stars of heaven and threw them to the earth." The stars are the angels that were cast out of heaven with him. Satan lost everything that he had when he was cast out of heaven. God tore out the precious stones and replaced them with scales. The anointed cherub who covers became a great dragon who deceives.

Now we know who Satan is and how he became our enemy but we must understand why he fights against us. This will also help us to understand more of who we are to be. As Satan, we were also created to worship and boast about God. 1 Corinthians 1:31 says, "that, as it is written, "He who glories, let him glory in the Lord." This same thing is said in 2 Corinthians 10:17. We are to worship God and give Him all the glory. Our job is to stand in His presence. Jude 1:24 says, "Now to Him who is able to keep you from stumbling, and to present you faultless before the presence of His glory with exceeding joy." He is going to present us without sin in His presence. Psalms 24:3-4 says, "Who may ascend into the hill of the Lord? Or who may stand in His holy place? He who has clean hands and a pure heart, who has not lifted up his soul to an idol, nor sworn deceitfully." We know that we are blameless and are pure because of Jesus' death on the cross. If we have surrendered our lives to Christ then we will stand in the presence of God. Our job is to reflect God's glory. 1 Peter 2:5 says, "You also, as living stones, are being built up a spiritual house, a holy priesthood, to offer up spiritual sacrifices acceptable to God through Jesus Christ." The living stones this verse talks about means the stones that Satan used to be covered in. They were to reflect God's glory and now we are to be as those stones on the earth. 2 Corinthians 3:18 says, "But we all, with unveiled faces, beholding as in a mirror the glory of the Lord, are being transformed into the same image from glory to glory, just as by the Spirit of the Lord." We are to be as a mirror showing the Shekinah Glory of God. Our final job is to make a joyful noise. Psalm 95:1 says, "Oh come, let us sing to the Lord! Let us shout joyfully to the Rock of our salvation." We are to praise God with everything in us. We were also created with instruments like Satan. The strings are our vocal chords. The pipes are our lungs. The percussion our hands and feet. We are now the ones that are to be the worshipers of God. Satan hates this because he does not want God to be worshipped. In the Garden of Eden, Adam and Eve could worship God faultlessly because they were perfect. Satan then deceived Eve to eat the fruit of the only tree that God had forbidden them to eat from as recorded in Genesis 3. She also gave some to Adam and he ate. Because we rebelled against God like the devil, this world is in a fallen state and there is still a great war going on against all those that have surrendered their lives to Christ. Satan does not care about how many times you sin or how much evil you do. All he wants is for you to not worship God. He will get us to worship anything but God. Many of us worship movies, video games, sports, music, girls, guys, and even the church. We must be sure that we are directing all our worship to God. This is one way that we can fight Satan. We must do our job correctly instead of letting him distract us from our purpose. Our job is demonstrated by the High Priest in Leviticus. The High Priest was the facilitator of worship. He would wear a breastplate that was adorned with twelve stones and nine of them were the stones that covered Satan. The High priest was the only on that could wear it. He was also the only one that could enter the Holy of Holies, which is the presence of God. When the High Priest would enter the Holy of Holies, the Shekinah Glory of God would reflect off the stones on the breastplate. Now because of Jesus' death, we are all able to be High priests and can enter in to the presence of God. We also do not need the breast plate of stones but are to reflect the glory of God with our lives. This is our purpose and this is what Satan will attack most. We need to be true worshippers of God and stand up to fight against Satan and not back down. We need to be the worshippers who worship in Spirit and truth. We need to be the holy priesthood of God. We need to worship God alone and that is the war we wage.

CHAPTER 3

The Beginning of the War

In this chapter we are going to look at the very beginning of this war and the first sin that led to it. First, we need to start at creation. Genesis 1-2 explains the entire creation but does not tell us when He created the angels. It does tell us when He created the first heaven though. There are three different heavens. In 2 Corinthians 12:2, Paul says, "I know a man in Christ who fourteen years ago whether in the body I do not know, or whether out of the body I do not know, God knows such a one was caught up to the third heaven." In this Scripture Paul is talking about himself and says that he went to the third heaven, which is where God lives. The first heaven was created on the second day. Genesis 1:6-8 says, Then God said, "Let there be a firmament in the midst of the waters, and let it divide the waters from the waters."

Thus God made the firmament, and divided the waters which were under the firmament from the waters which were above the firmament; and it was so. And God called the firmament heaven. So evening and morning were the second day. Many people try to say that the firmament is really the ground, but Genesis 1:20 says, "Then God said, "Let the waters abound with an abundance of living creatures, and let birds fly above the earth across the face of the firmament." Just so you know birds do not fly in the ground. This means that the firmament is the sky. It also says that it divides the water below it from the water above it. This means that at the beginning there was a layer of water above the earth which would have actually protected all life from the harmful rays of the sun and would cause a greenhouse effect. This is why humans were able to live close to a thousand years in the beginning. This was when the first heaven was made. Then Genesis 1:14-17 says, "Then God said, "Let there be lights in the firmaments in the midst of the heavens to divide the day from the night; and let them be for signs and seasons, and for days and years; and let them be for lights in the firmament of the heavens to give light on the earth", and it was so. Then God made two great lights: the greater light to rule the day and the lesser light to rule the night. He made the stars also. God set the stars in the heavens to give light on the earth." This means that the first heaven is in our atmosphere. The second heaven is the rest of the universe. The third heaven is unseen and is the place where God lives and is the heaven we go to when we die. This was all created on the fourth day which means that all three heavens were created before this day and all the angels were created too. This is where Satan had his beginning. It was sometime on the second, third, or fourth day. We do not know exactly when He became prideful and rebelled but we do know that it was after all the days of creation. Genesis 1:31 says "Then God saw everything that He had made, and indeed it was very good. So evening and morning were the sixth day." It was said that it was good so there was no sin and nothing wrong with any of the creation. This means that Satan must have fallen from heaven sometime after the seventh day. All we know is that he was cast out of heaven to the earth and the first thing he did was deceive Eve to sin. God made Adam on the sixth day. Genesis 2:16-17 says, "And the Lord God commanded the man, saying, "Of every tree of the garden you may freely eat but of the tree of the knowledge of good and evil you may not eat, for in the day that you eat of it you shall surely die." After this, God created Eve to be Adam's wife and she was told by Adam that it was forbidden to eat of the tree. Genesis 3 is when Satan first tempts anyone to break the command given by God. Satan questioned the woman about which tree she could eat and she said that they could eat of any tree except for the tree of the knowledge of good and evil and that they should not even touch it. God actually did not say that she should not touch it but that was what Adam told her. Adam gave some miscommunication which still got the point across, but it was not God's word. When we do not interpret the word of God to others correctly we can set them up to fall into sin in many ways. This was not a terrible miscommunication, but if Eve would have touched the fruit and seen that she did not die, then she would believe that God lied and that it was fine to eat. In Genesis 3:4-5 Satan replies saying, "You will not surely die. For God knows that in the day you eat of it your eyes will be opened, and you will be like God, knowing good and evil." Satan denied God's word and tempted them with what Satan truly wanted. He said that they could be like God. Satan wanted to be like God so he deceived us by saying that we could be like Him. He said that God was not giving them the best things and that there is so much more if we disobeyed Him. Since she did not die when she first touched it, she saw the tree was good for food and decided to eat it. Then Adam ate the fruit also and both their eyes were open to see that they were naked and became ashamed of it. Because they were ashamed, they hid themselves from God and when God came walking in the garden He called and asked Adam where he was. Adam answered and said, "I heard Your voice in the garden and I was afraid because I was naked and I hid myself." God replied, "Who told you that you were naked? Have you eaten of the tree from which I commanded you that you should not eat?" Many people say that Adam blamed the woman but if we look closer at the verse we can see who he really blamed. Adam replied saying, "The woman whom You gave to be with me, she gave me of the tree and I ate." He blamed God because He was the one that gave Eve to him and she was the first one to eat of it. Adam went from wanting to be like God to blaming Him for breaking His own commandments. Many people still do this. We say that if God did not want us to sin, then He would make it impossible for us to do such things or give us better strength to withstand all the temptations which we have. The truth is that God gives us all the strength we need through His Spirit but because of our free will we have the choice to sin or not. Adam and Eve both made the choice to sin against God on their own. Then God asked the woman, Eve, what she had done. She answered also blaming God saying, "The serpent that you put in the garden deceived me and I ate." The serpent that God put in the garden deceived her so because God put it in the garden then He must have wanted her to sin. People always do this with God. They blame Him for their own sins that they chose to commit because they are scared of the consequences and want to believe that they are good people that only do good things. That is not true though, because of the first sin we are inherently evil and will all commit sin in our lives. It is not because God caused us to sin but because Adam and Eve first sinned and by our free will we choose to sin. Then God gave punishment to the serpent, to Eve, and to Adam. God said to the serpent, "Because you have done this, you are more cursed than all the cattle, and more than every beast of the field; on your belly you shall go, and you shall eat dust all the days of your life. I will put enmity between you and the woman, and between your seed and her seed; he shall bruise your head, and you shall bruise his heel." This is where Spiritual Warfare fully began. God told Satan that the seed of the woman would some day crush his head and have victory over him. This was fulfilled with Jesus when He died on the cross. The devil thought that he had won but instead Jesus had truly conquered the grave and defeated the devil. In the next chapter I will go into more detail about this subject. Then God said to the woman, "I will greatly multiply your sorrow and your conception; in pain you shall bring forth children; your desire shall be for your husband, and he shall rule over you." Because of Eve's sin women go through great pain while giving birth and the man is ruler over her. Before sin, the woman was the helper to the man and was at equal standing but because of sin, the man is now higher than the woman. They were both called Adam. Until the sin Eve was just called the woman and they were considered one flesh and person. Now she is considered separate because of this sin. In marriage, the parents should be equal because that is how God designed it, with each having different roles but still being one flesh. Many marriages do accomplish having each other be equal and it is great but it would have been completely natural if Eve did not sin. Finally God said to Adam, "Cursed is the ground for your sake; in toil you shall eat of it all the days of your life. Both thorns and thistles it shall bring forth for you, and you shall eat the herb of the field. In the sweat of your face you shall eat bread till you return to the ground, for out of it you were taken; for dust you are, and to dust you shall return." Because of the first sin, work is actually tiresome and is hard for us. Before sin it was pleasurable and everything was enjoyable. Now there are many things wrong with the world that harm us and are not pleasurable. Then Adam and Eve were driven out of the garden and were never allowed to enter it again because of the sin they committed. Some people say that God did lie because Adam and Eve did not die as soon as they ate the fruit but they truly did. When they ate the fruit they immediately made this world a broken world and death entered the world. Before sin there was no such thing as death and they had true life. Now we live in a fallen state and are truly in a dead state because we are growing closer to dying every second. They were thrown into a dying state as soon as they ate of the fruit. This is where it all fully began. It did begin in heaven when Satan became prideful and rebelled against God but we were brought into the war because of Adam and Eve's sin.

Now I want discuss a theory that I have. By saying this is a theory, I am stating that there is no absolute way to prove this but I do believe that there is truth in it and that it is a very good thing to at least think about. 1 Timothy 2:14 says, "And Adam was not deceived, but the woman being deceived, fell into transgression. The question this verse poses is that if Adam was not deceived then why did he sin? The definition of the word used here is to be tricked into doing something that is wrong. Basically this means that Adam knew it was wrong. I believe that Adam sinned, knowing that it was wrong, to save his wife, Eve. When Eve ate the fruit, Adam knew that she was going to be punished with death. Adam did not protect her from the serpent and he did things that were wrong, but he did know that they were not to eat the fruit. Because of this, I believe Adam decided to eat it with her so he would not to lose her. He knew that she would die and God would just make another like her for him but Adam loved Eve. He loved her so much that he did not want a different person but truly her. He believed that if they both sinned then God would in some way redeem them both and he could still be with Eve. That is what God did. God could have killed them both and created a new species just like them, but He loved them so much that he decided to save them. He didn't want some different form like them but truly them. He loved us even though we disobeyed Him and then He sent Jesus to die in our place for our sin. If we believe that Jesus died for us then we are redeemed and are able to be with God forever. As I said, it is impossible to completely prove this theory, but it does show us the greatness of God's love and why He decided to save us. Thank you, Lord for your amazing love and grace.

CHAPTER 4

The History of the War

It is time to look at the events of Spiritual Warfare shown in the Bible. I will not look at every event but will cover most of them. In Genesis 3:15 God says, "And I will put enmity between you and the woman, and between your seed and her seed; He shall bruise your head, and you shall bruise his heel." This means that at some time there would be a descendant of Eve who will overcome the devil and crush his head. All of the Spiritual Warfare in the Old Testament is about the devil trying to get rid of the descendant that will defeat him. The two ways he does this is through death and making them sin. If they sin, then they cannot overcome the devil.

Genesis 4 gives the account of the first sons of Eve. The first one was Cain and the second was Abel. Because

Satan knows that a descendant of Eve will crush him, he starts to work on Cain. They both gave an offering to the Lord but Cain's offering was half-hearted and Abel's offering was the best. Then Cain became very angry and was driven to kill Abel. This would have worked because the righteous one was killed and Cain and his descendants were cursed. This did not work though because Eve gave birth to Seth.

Later, Genesis 6:1-3 says, "Now it came to pass, when men began to multiply on the face of the earth, and daughters were born to them, that the sons of God saw the daughters of men were beautiful; and they took wives for themselves of all whom they chose. And the Lord said, "My Spirit shall not strive with man forever, for he is indeed flesh; yet his days shall be one hundred and twenty years." The sons of God are actually fallen angels. These are demons that came and took wives and then they bore children that were half human and half angelic. Verse 5-7 says, "Then the Lord saw that the wickedness of man was great in the earth, and that every intent of the thoughts of his heart was only evil continually. And the Lord was sorry that He had made man on the earth, and He was grieved in His heart. So the Lord said, "I will destroy man whom I have created from the face of the earth, both man and beast, creeping thing and birds of the air, for I am sorry that I have made them." God was grieved that this was happening to His favorite creation and He knew that this could not continue. He had to destroy the human race but there was one man that was still righteous. Verse 8-9 says, "But Noah found grace in the eyes of the Lord. This is the genealogy of Noah. Noah was a just man, perfect in his generations. Noah walked with God." By saying that Noah was perfect in his generations it means that demons did not have any wives in his family and he was purely flesh. Because of this he was just and able to walk with God. God decided to save Noah and his family and two of every animal on the earth. God caused a great flood to cover the entire earth and directed Noah to build an ark to house his family and two, male and female, of every animal while the rest of creation was killed by the flood.

Then in Genesis 18 Abraham, who was promised by God to be the father of many nations, had an encounter with three angels. Verses 20-21 say, "And the Lord said, 'Because the outcry against Sodom and Gomorrah is great, and because their sin is very grave, I will go down now and see whether they have done altogether according to the outcry against it that has come to Me; and if not I will know.'" The Lord sent these angels to check and see if what was told about Sodom and Gomorrah was true. On their way they stopped and spent time with Abraham. The outcry against Sodom and Gomorrah was that men were having sex with other men. After the angels departed from Abraham, he went to the Lord and had a conversation with God where God promised that He would not destroy the entire city if there were at least ten people that were righteous. The angels then went to Sodom and spent the night at Lot's house. While there, the men of the city, both young and old, came to the house and asked Lot where the men were that came to him that night. They told Lot to bring them out so that they may know them carnally. The word "know" in this verse, and most other verses in the Old Testament, means to have sex. They were asking to have sex with the angels that were in Lot's house. By this it was shown that the outcry against Sodom and Gomorrah was true. Also there were not even ten people that were found righteous anywhere in the city. This is most likely where AIDS first started and it was probably threatening to wipe out all the people in the world. If not AIDS, then at least some other very deadly disease. Because of this, God destroyed Sodom and Gomorrah but told Lot so that his family could leave the city and live.

After all of this, Abraham had a son and his name was Isaac. This was the only son he had and he loved him very much. It was at this time that God decided to test Abraham. Genesis 22:2 says, "Then He said, 'Take now your son, your only son Isaac, whom you love, and go to the land of Moriah, and offer him there as a burnt offering on one of the mountains on which I will tell you.'" During this time in history, it was actually common to sacrifice children to gods. The test that God gave Abraham was to see if he would still follow him even when it meant killing his only son. It also shows that God is not like any of the other made up gods. Genesis 22:10-12 says, "And Abraham stretched out his hand and took the knife to slay his son. But the angel of the Lord called to him from heaven and said, 'Abraham, Abraham!' So he said, 'Here I am.' And He said, 'Do not lay your hand on the lad, or do anything to him; for now I know that you fear God, since you have not withheld your son, your only son, from Me.'" God saved Abraham's son and gave a lamb for the offering. This shows that God is not like any other god. He did not take the sacrifice of children but provided His own sacrifice for Abraham.

Isaac then had Jacob and Esau, and Jacob had twelve sons and one of them was named Joseph. The story of Joseph is told in Genesis 37-50. Joseph was loved by his father more than all the others and because of this the other brothers hated him. Joseph then had two dreams which signified that all his brothers and parents would bow down to him. Then one day Joseph went out and met his brothers and they had plotted to kill him but Judah, one of the brothers pleaded that they throw him in a pit so that he could later come back and save him out of the pit. They agreed to throw him in the pit. Meanwhile, there were some Ishmaelites heading to Egypt and the brothers decided to sell Joseph to them as a slave. They sold him, and took his tunic and dipped it in the blood of a sheep and took it back to Jacob and said that he must have been killed by some animal. When Joseph came to Egypt he was sold to Potiphar, who was an officer of Pharaoh. The Lord was with Joseph and he had him prosper in whatever he did. Joseph found favor in Potiphar's sight so he made Joseph overseer of his entire house. Then Potiphar's wife wanted Joseph and came to him at times and asked him to sleep with her. One of these times she grabbed him by his shirt and he ran from her but she tore off his shirt as he ran. Then she showed her husband the shirt and said that Joseph came and raped her, so Potiphar had him thrown in prison. After a while the keeper of the prison committed Joseph to be the head overseer of the prison while still being a prisoner. In this position, Joseph had complete control over everything that happened in the prison. Then one day two of the prisoners had dreams that they did not understand. Joseph offered to interpret them. The first one was of the former butler of Pharaoh and he told Joseph his dream and Joseph said that it meant that in three days he would be restored to his prior position. Then the former baker told Joseph his dream and Joseph said that it meant that in three days he would be killed. These interpretations came true and the butler was restored to being Pharaoh's butler and the baker was killed. Then two years later Pharaoh had two dreams that he could not understand and none of the wise men could interpret them for him. The butler then remembered Joseph and told Pharaoh that he could interpret the dreams. He had Joseph brought to him and told him the dreams and Joseph said that the dreams meant there would be seven years of plenty for the harvest and then seven years of famine that could kill almost everyone if there was not enough food. Pharaoh then asked Joseph how to make sure they could survive. He made a plan and Pharaoh appointed Joseph over all the people to make sure that his plan was kept and that everyone would live. The seven years of famine came and Jacob sent his sons to Egypt to get grain and they came to Joseph and bowed to him but they did not recognize him. They then told Joseph about their family and that Jacob had another son named Benjamin. Joseph accused them of being spies and asked them to go back and bring the youngest brother with them next time to prove that they were not spies. After they ran out of the grain they got from Joseph they decided to go back to Egypt and had to bring their brother Benjamin this time. When they came to Egypt they showed how they had brought Benjamin. Joseph said that they were not guilty of being spies and gave them grain but had his own silver cup placed in Benjamin's sack without the brothers knowing. Then Joseph had men follow them and accuse them of stealing the cup. Because of this Benjamin was to be killed but Judah said that he would take the place of Benjamin because he know his father could not bear to lose another son. Then Joseph could not restrain himself anymore and he showed the brothers that it was him and asked them to bring his father to Egypt and they would all come and live in Egypt. They brought Jacob and they prospered in Egypt for many years and had many descendants that lived in.

After many years, Egypt had a new king rise up and he saw that the Israelites, the descendants of Jacob, were greater and mightier than the Egyptians. He was then scared that they may join with their enemies to overthrow them so he made them all slaves and afflicted them greatly. He decided that all the sons should be killed so that the daughters would be forced to marry Egyptians and the Israelites would no longer be a race on the earth. Then all the sons of the Israelites were killed. But one of the mothers made a small ark and placed her son, whose name is Moses, in it and sent it down the river. It was then found by the king's daughter and she was able to keep him and raise him as her own. Years later, Moses saw the burdens that the Egyptians cast upon the Israelites. One day he saw an Egyptian beating and Israelite so he killed the Egyptian. When the king heard of this he sought to kill Moses so Moses fled to Midian and married one of the daughters of the priest of Midian. He worked as a shepherd for his father-in-law named Jethro and one day when he was tending to the flock, Moses came upon a burning bush. Out of the bush the Lord spoke to him and told him that he was to deliver the Israelites out of the hand of the Egyptians and lead them to a place that was flowing with milk and honey. He was told to go to the king of Egypt and ask for the Israelites to be let go and that if the king refused then he would send many plagues on Egypt. Moses went to the king and the king refused, so the Lord sent a plague on Egypt for every time the king refused. The king refused ten times until the last plague happened in which all the Israelites would kill a lamb and put the blood on the doorpost. That night the angel of death would come and kill all the firstborn of the families that did not have the blood of the lamb on the doorpost. After this the king was very grieved and he let the people of Israel go. Moses then led the Israelites away from Egypt but the king then decided to chase after and kill them for all that had happened because of them. When they came to the Red Sea, Moses lifted his staff and the waters parted before him and the Israelites went across it on dry land and they waited for the king and Egyptians to get in the middle of the sea and then he let the water fall on them and crushed them all. The rest of the book of Exodus through Deuteronomy is about the law. This is where the Ten Commandments were given and the instructions for the Tabernacle. They wandered in the desert for forty years until Moses died and Joshua was chosen by God to lead them into the Promised Land that the Lord said would be given into their hand.

They were led by Joshua into the Promised Land and overtook all the armies of the nations which had occupied the land. They took the land and it was the birthplace of the nation of Israel. The the book of Judges is all about how Israel revolted against the Lord and served other gods and because of this the Lord had Israel taken captive by the other nations around them. The Lord raised up judges for every generation that would deliver them out of their captivity and then judge and lead the nation. One of these judges was Samson and he was to release Israel from the Philistines but disobeyed God because he was told not to eat or drink anything that pertains to wine, not to touch dead animals, and to never cut his hair. When he obeyed these he had great strength but he disobeyed them all and lost his strength. Then the Philistines took him and plucked his eyes out and had him chained between two pillars for all the Philistines to see at a banquet and they mocked him. Then Samson cried out to God for his strength to be restored so that he could destroy the Philistines and free Israel. The Lord gave him his strength back and he tore down the pillars and they fell on the Philistines and killed them all.

First and Second Samuel is the account of the first kings of Israel. The Israelites cried out to Samuel, who was the High Priest, to give them a king so they could be like all the other nations. God was angry against them for this, but he led Samuel to find Saul who became the first king of Israel. Then Saul did evil in the sight of the Lord. When they were about to attack another nation, they were waiting for Samuel to arrive so that he could give a sacrifice to God so that they would win. Samuel was late getting there so Saul decided that he would make the sacrifice but it was against the commandments of God because only the High Priest was to give the sacrifices. When Samuel heard of this he went and told Saul that the kingdom would be taken from him and given to another who was a man after God's own heart.

Saul also did more evil against the Lord because he was commanded to utterly destroy the Amalekites but instead he kept their king and all the livestock. Samuel was led by God to the house of Jesse where he found David and anointed him to be king of Israel after Saul's death. After he was anointed king he went to where the Israelites were to be fighting the Philistines. But no one there wanted to fight Goliath who was a giant. David saw Goliath and heard him blaspheme the name of the Lord and no one would attempt to fight him. He then decided that he would fight Goliath and he went up against him with a sling and a stone. He knew that the Lord would destroy Goliath through him and when he slung the stone at Goliath it hit him and the Bible says it sank deeply into his head. He took Goliath's own sword and cut the giants head off with it. After this Saul became angry with David because all the Israelites loved David more than him, and he knew that David was to be the one that would take over his throne. So he sought to kill David, but David escaped him and during the time Saul was seeking him, David had the opportunity to kill him twice but he swore that he would not kill the Lord's anointed. After Saul died in battle, David became king over Israel.

Later, David sinned against God because he slept with Bathsheba who was the wife of Uriah, one of the commanders of his army. Bathsheba became pregnant and David had Uriah killed in battle and took Bathsheba as his wife to hide that he had slept with her while Uriah was gone to war. Then the Lord sent Nathan to David and he spoke to David of how he sinned and David paid for his sin by losing four of his children, but the Lord still called him a man after God's own heart. Israel then had many kings but many of them did evil against God and in the book of Esther most of the Israelites were under the rule of King Ahasuerus, which is translated into Greek as Xerxes. He was the evil king in the movie *300*. In Esther the right hand man for Xerxes was Haman and he hated the Israelites because of Mordecai who raised Esther after her parents had been killed. Haman had a decree made that ordered all the Israelites to be killed. Haman was basically the first Hitler. When Mordecai heard of it he went to Ester and told her that she had to try and stop it. She had the king and Haman come to a banquet twice. At the second one she told the king that she was an Israelite and that Haman had ordered to have her and all her people killed. Xerxes was extremely angry at Haman for doing this because Esther was his wife, so he canceled the decree and killed Haman and all his family. She saved the nation of Israel.

The rest of the Old Testament focuses on the prophets and everything that happened in the nation of Israel. There are many other times that Israel was taken captive and had been rescued and restored but I am going to skip these and go to the New Testament. You can read of this in the Old Testament if you want to make sure that this all truly happened.

The beginning of the New Testament is all about Jesus' life. He was the seed of the woman that would crush Satan's head. Throughout his life he was tempted in every way but did not sin, so he was the only one able to defeat the devil. He taught of the kingdom of God and cast out demons and performed many miracles. Satan knew that he had to destroy him somehow so he used Judas, one of Jesus' disciples, to betray him to Roman guards who took him where he was run through trials. They decided that he should be crucified and cried out to Pilate, a Roman commander, to have him crucified. He had Jesus whipped mercilessly and then ordered him to be crucified. Jesus carried his cross to the place of crucifixion and He was crucified and died. It looked like the devil had finally won but he was wrong. Because Jesus had not sinned in any way, he was wrongly crucified and was the only person able to overcome Satan and he has the victory. Jesus was promised to come from the nation of Israel and the line of Judah. Throughout the Old Testament Satan had tried to destroy Israel and corrupt the line so that Jesus would not be able to defeat him, but Jesus did defeat him with His death and resurrection. The battle is won. We still fight Spiritual Warfare because he is not destroyed but we must understand that Satan has been conquered and through Christ we are more than conquerors. Now, Satan does warfare differently. He knows he is defeated but he still wants to lead people away from God and kill the people that love Him. Satan has done this through wars, Hitler, 9/11, other religions, and sin that entangles us. We need to know and understand all this so that we see his game plan. The following parts of this book are going to focus on exactly what we can do to make sure we do not fall victim to his schemes. But the main thing we must understand is that Satan is defeated and even if we fall, God will cleanse us from our sins and make us pure so that we can still overcome the devil. God supplied his own sacrifice when he asked Abraham to sacrifice his son and he has supplied it through Jesus so that we can be cleansed from our sin. This is the history of the war and Jesus was and is and will always be the over comer.

CHAPTER 5

Belt of Truth

We have looked at where this war began, how it has played out in history and the way it works today. Now it is time to go deep into how to defend ourselves using the armor of God that is given to us in the Bible. Ephesians 6:10-18 is the passage that we will be going through during the next few chapters to cover everything that we must have to defend ourselves. It says, "Finally, my brethren, be strong in the Lord and in the power of His might. Put on the whole armor of God that you may be able to stand against the wiles of the devil. For we do not wrestle against flesh and blood, but against principalities, against powers, against the rulers of the darkness of this age, against spiritual hosts of wickedness in the heavenly places. Therefore take up the whole armor of God that you may be able to stand in the evil day, and having done all to stand. Stand therefore, having girded your waist with truth, having put on the breastplate of righteousness, and having shod your feet with the preparation of the gospel of peace; above all, taking the shield of faith with which you will be able to quench all the fiery darts of the wicked one. And take the helmet of salvation, and the sword of the Spirit, which is the word of God; praying always with all prayer and supplication for all the saints." Verse 13 says that we must have the whole armor of God to be able to stand in the evil day. There is no soldier in the world that would go out into battle without having everything that he needs. Many Christians believe that if they have most of the armor, then they will be okay and might make it through everything that will come at them. That is not true. This says that we need the whole armor of God to be able to stand. Every piece is just as important as the others. We need it all. It also says that we need it to stand in the evil day. Most preachers teach that this is talking about the last days, which is still good, but everyone on the earth will have an evil day even if we do not live until Christ comes back. We need to put this armor on every day so that we are prepared to stand against whatever the devil throws at us.

Paul wrote Ephesians while he was under house arrest. This means that he was actually chained to a

Roman guard while he was writing this letter. This Roman guard would be in full armor every day to be ready for anything that would happen even if he was just watching one person. The Roman guards were trained to always be ready for anything because they never truly knew what a day may bring forth. This is how we must be; always dressed in full armor ready for anything that could happen even if we doubt that we will be attacked that day. We never know how a day will play out so we must be ready to stand firm always. Since Paul was chained to this guard every day, he probably used the armor the guard was wearing to illustrate the armor of God. The first piece of armor mentioned is the belt of truth. The beginning of verse 14 says, "Stand therefore, having girded your waist with truth." The belt that a soldier would wear was made to hold everything else in place. It kept the rest of the armor exactly how it should be. It was also the first part to be put on. When soldiers went out to fight they would tuck in the bottom of whatever they were wearing into the belt so that they could easily access their sword and everything else they may need. This piece of armor represents truth because lies are one of the main tactics of the devil. There are four main areas that the devil lies about.

The first area is God. The devil will mainly lie about God's existence and character. The world has been covered with so many different religions and beliefs in other gods, but one of the largest non-truths that is the believed is that we evolved over millions of years. Everything in evolution is exactly opposite of what the Bible teaches. The Bible says that there is a God who created us and loves us. Evolution says that we are just an accident and can become our own God. The Bible says that man brought death into the world by our sin. Evolution says that the death of animals over billions of years brought man into the world. It is the exact opposite of the Bible and it has led many people to believe that there is no God. It says that everything in life is an accident and that we are all just animals. This belief has ruined millions of people's lives and has led to the entire extermination of millions. People have died simply because they believed that there was a God. In the Columbine shooting the two shooters asked a girl named Cassie if she believed in a God. When she said yes, they shot her in the head. Hitler tried to kill all of the Jews because he believed that they were the least evolved and he thought that if he could kill off all the lesser races then evolution would speed up. Hitler wanted to be his own God. Evolution is taught in every public school in the country and is basically being shoved down every student's throat. Hitler once said, "If you tell a lie long enough, loud enough, and often enough the people will believe it." That is exactly what has been done with evolution. Another lie about God has to do with His character. The devil used this at the first sin. He told Eve that God knows in the day that they eat of the fruit they will be as God. He told Eve that God was holding out on her and not wanting her to be like Him. Truly God loves us more than we could ever comprehend or even imagine. He wants to give us blessings and lead us to whatever is best for us. So many Christians do not always believe that God cares about them or that they are being heard by Him. This leads us to try and do everything on our own which is exactly what the devil wants to happen because we cannot do anything on our own. God is the only reason that we are alive today. He is the only reason you exist. He loves you and loves taking care of you but you must trust that He will. So many people get scared because they have no direction, but they haven't even asked Him for direction. One thing that we must understand is that we should not be scared of being outside of God's will but always trust that He is leading us to His will. This is the truth about God's character and we must hold onto it so that the devil will not deceive us with these lies.

The second area the devil lies about is ourselves. The main way he lies about us is to make us question if we are really saved or not. He will point at all our wrongs and tell us that we would be saved if we didn't have so much sin. He makes us feel that if we just sin one more time, then we will lose our salvation. The truth is that we can't lose our salvation. If we have truly given over our lives to Jesus then he lives in us and God sees us as His perfect and holy Son. The only way that we are not saved is if we accept Jesus but do not repent and attempt to turn away from the sin that we are committing. We may still sin in the same way at times but our heart must be changed to where we do not desire to keep sinning. The only sin that the Bible says is unforgivable is the blaspheming of the Holy Spirit. Mark 3:29 says, "But he who blasphemes against the Holy Spirit never has forgiveness, but is subject to eternal condemnation." The blaspheming of the Holy Spirit is when the Spirit convicts you of your sin and you know that you need God but turn away from Him. That is the only sin that God will not forgive you of. The devil also makes us believe that if we were saved then we would not have thoughts about these sins. Truly that is most likely temptation to sin. Being tempted and sinning are completely different. We will have thoughts about sinning but we do not need to sin. Jesus was also tempted on this earth. Hebrews 4:15 says, "For we do not have a High Priest who cannot sympathize with our weaknesses, but was in all points tempted as we are, yet without sin." Jesus was tempted in every way that the whole world has been yet was able to restrain himself from sinning. It is normal to be tempted but we do not need to sin. Yes, we will still sin, but if our desire is to turn from sin, then we are followers of Jesus Christ because our heart is after what He wishes for us.

The third area that the devil lies to us about is our worth. He lies by saying that we are unworthy of everything that God has given us. This makes us believe that we are inadequate of being a son of God and that we do not deserve to be followers of Christ. The main times that we are set back in our faith is when we have questions about our worthiness. This happens many times throughout Scripture. Moses thought that he was unworthy because he stuttered when he spoke. Gideon felt unworthy because he was hiding while the city was being taken over. Saul felt that he was unworthy to be king over Israel, and because of that he was led into sin that cost him the kingdom. We need to know that we are worth everything. Jesus died just for you meaning that if you were the only person that would be saved by His death, then He would have still died. You are worth everything to Him. You are also worthy of everything that He has called you to be. He has a specific plan and purpose for your life and this lie is the only thing that will make you unable to achieve it. You are worthy of being a son of God. Never doubt it.

The fourth lie is that the devil lies to us about others. Many times we rejoice over others' failures because we believe that we are better than them. At times we can become jealous of someone else because they are better than us at a certain thing. Then if we hear that they failed at something or are not good enough, we rejoice by believing that we are much better than they are. We can also do this with sin. Satan can cause us to believe that someone we know is trapped in a sin and we believe that because we do not sin in that way then we are better Christians. The truth is that we are all sinners and all sin is the same. We cannot look at anyone's sin and believe that we are better than them because we only see a little of their sin and yet our sin is so much more. Matthew 7:3-5 says, "And why do you look at the speck in your brother's eye, but do not consider the plank in your own eye? "Or how can you say to your brother, 'Let me remove the speck from your eye'; and look, a plank is in your own eye? "Hypocrite! First remove the plank from your own eye, and then you will see clearly to remove the speck from your brother's eye." Unless we are completely free from sin we cannot look at others as being worse than ourselves. Instead we should join with others and help each other overcome the sin in both of our lives instead of just pointing at each other's. We also look at people with more authority than us sinning, and feel it is ok for us to sin as well. For example, I never understood why many policeman do not follow their own laws. A lot of them park where we are told not to and they are always on a computer in their car while we are not even supposed to talk on the phone while driving. We can look at things like this and believe that we do not need to follow these laws, but where sin in concerned, no matter who is doing it, everyone will be judged the same by God. We cannot blame anyone else for making our sin right in our eyes because we have been told it is wrong by the Word of God. We can also believe that spiritual leaders have worse sin than us. I was apart of a church once where the pastor's wife actually had breast enhancement surgery done. That is a sin by making others lust after her. There is truly no other reason to have that kind of surgery. We see that and then believe because we are better than the pastor we should not worry about our own sin. That is a lie. They will be judged the same as we are. The devil tells us these lies just to make us feel like our sin is not bad so we will continue in it. But truly it is despicable and will damage your relationship with God. In John 14:15 Jesus says, "If you love Me, keep my commandments." If we truly love God, then we would show it through our actions by following what He wishes. He wishes us to not sin against Him so we should not do it. Sin will still happen but let's not believe these lies that make it seem okay for ourselves to continue sinning.

These four areas discussed are the main ones told by the devil, but any lie will push us back and damage us. We must hold tightly to all truth because a lie is from the devil. The end of John 8:44 says, talking about the devil, "For he is a liar and the father of it." He is the father of all lies so every lie comes from him. This is the first piece of armor that we must have to overcome the devil.

CHAPTER 6

Breastplate of Righteousness

In this chapter I will discuss the second half of Ephesians 6:14, "Having put on the breastplate of righteousness." The main point of this chapter is to understand that if God fights for me then I will not fall. 2 Corinthians 4:7-10 demonstrates this by saying, "But we have this treasure in earthen vessels, that the excellence of the power may be of God and not of us. We are hard-pressed on every side, yet not crushed; we are perplexed, but not in despair; persecuted, but not forsaken; struck down, but not destroyed, always carrying about in the body the dying of the Lord Jesus, that the life of Jesus also may be manifested in our body." Romans 8:31b also says, "If God is for us, who can be against us?" If God is fighting for us then we can stand firm knowing that there is nothing in the physical world and even the spiritual world that can defeat us.

In this scripture the breastplate is actually a garment under the rest of the armor called chainmail. This garment is shown in *Lord of the Rings the Two Towers.* If you remember right before the battle at Helms deep, Gimli the dwarf comes out and is trying to fit into the chainmail and it is very tight around his stomach and he can barely get it around himself. That is what chainmail is. It is basically just a lot of small circular metal linked together to make an entire suit. Without this chainmail, swords would easily cut straight through people. We can have the larger armor around us, but without the chainmail, a small knick would cut us. This helps to stop the sword from completely cutting straight through us. This is the only thing that can completely guard our entire body.

Now we need to understand how to put on the breastplate of righteousness. Most of the time we are only fighting in the flesh. To have this breastplate we need to fight in the power of God. Remember this is a spiritual battle which means that we must fight in the spirit realm. If we are only fighting in the physical then we are having a negative effect in the spirit world. Isaiah 41:10 says, "Fear not, for I am with you; be not dismayed, for I am your God. I will strengthen you, yes,

I will help you. I will uphold you with my righteous right hand." God tells us that he will fight for us with his righteous right hand. The only way to be victorious is by righteousness. Luke 22:69 says, "Hereafter the Son of Man will sit on the right hand of the power of God." Jesus Christ is the one that is sitting at the right hand of God which means that it is His righteousness we need. To understand how we can get Jesus' righteousness we need to go back to the very beginning of Genesis.

Adam and Eve were the first people to ever be created by God and it says that God decided to create them in His image. This does not mean that they look exactly like God but that they had part of the same nature. They were relational creatures and at the beginning, they were righteous. God is completely righteous and can never do anything wrong. We were created to have that kind of righteousness in us but God gave us a choice. He let us choose to follow Him by obeying his command to not eat of the tree of the knowledge of good and evil or to rebel and eat of it. When they ate of the fruit of that tree they automatically became unrighteous. Not only were they unrighteous but it became a part of our nature to be unrighteous and it was passed down to every person that would ever live. Psalm 51:5 says, "Behold, I was brought forth in iniquity, and in sin my mother conceived me." This means that even from conception we are unrighteous. Romans 3:23 says, "For all have sinned and fall short of the glory of God." We are no longer righteous but we were meant to be righteous. We all truly know that we are supposed to be righteous but are not, so we try to make ourselves righteous. This is called self-righteousness. There are two main ways that we try to do this. The first is through morality. A lot of us believe that if we are morally good people, then we will be considered righteous. Truly this does not help because it bases righteousness on the works that we do and if we do only one thing wrong then we are still unrighteous morally. Morality cannot make us righteous. The other way is through religion. Christianity is not religion. Christianity is a relationship between us and God. Religion truly is us being good so that God will accept us. Basically religion says I obey God so that He will bless me, while Christianity says God has already blessed me, therefore I obey. Religion is the direct opposite of Christianity. We can also never be completely righteous in religion. Neither of these can make us righteous so we need to have it given to us. This is where Jesus comes in. God sent Jesus to live on this earth and throughout His life He never sinned. Jesus was completely righteous. When Jesus died, He took all our unrighteousness on Himself and gave us His righteousness. 1 Peter 2:24 says talking about Jesus, "who Himself bore our sins in His body on the tree, that we, having died to sin, might live for righteousness by whose stripes you were healed." Phil 4:9 says, "and be found in Him, not having my own righteousness, which is from the law, but that which is through faith in Christ, the righteousness which is from God by faith." By Jesus' death we are dead to sin and are able to have His righteousness. If you have surrendered your life to Christ and He lives inside of you, then you have the righteousness of Jesus. This is called imputed righteousness. Isaiah 59:16-17 says, "He saw that there was no man, and wondered that there was no intercessor; therefore His own arm brought salvation for Him; and His own righteousness, it sustained Him. He put on righteousness as a breastplate, and a helmet of salvation upon His head; He put on the garments of vengeance for clothing, and was clad with zeal as a cloak." In this passage God is looking for a man that would intercede and stand in the gap for His people to help lead them to Him. He needed a warrior that would defeat the devil and bring salvation to all. It says that He found no one so He sent His own son to come and be the warrior. Christ was the first one to wear the full armor of God. It says in this passage that He wore the breastplate of righteousness and helmet of salvation. He is the only one that could defeat the devil and bring salvation to all. If we are saved, then we have Him living inside of us so we can now be the warrior that He was. By Jesus living inside of us we can stand as a warrior against Satan and fight for the people of this earth and the people of God. That is our mission; to stand and fight against the enemy and throughout this fight we lead people to know God. It is only by imputed righteousness that we have the power to do this.

A great example of this imputed righteousness (or power) is found in 1 Samuel 17. This is the story of David and Goliath. In this story Israel and the Philistines are going to war against each other but to prevent many of each army from being killed they decide to each send one champion to fight against each other and whoever wins is the victor of the war. The Philistine's champion was named Goliath, a giant who was about ten feet tall. Saul and the men of Israel were greatly afraid of Goliath and no one went out to fight Him. Because of this, Goliath mocked the armies of Israel and God because the people did not believe that God would give them the power to win. For forty days Goliath would stand in front of the army of Israel and mock them. David was the youngest of eight brothers born to the man Jesse. Jesse's three oldest sons were a part of the army of Israel and Jesse asked David to take some food to his brothers. So David went and found his brothers and they told him about the Philistine. David saw Goliath and heard him mocking the armies of Israel and his God. He then asks, "Who is this uncircumcised Philistine that he should defy the armies of the living God." David then tells Saul that he will fight the Philistine. David was very young compared to the rest of the army of Israel so Saul did not believe that he could stand a chance against the Philistine. Then David told Saul about how when he was tending the sheep of his father, a lion and bear came and took one of the sheep and he killed them both with his bare hands. He says that Goliath will be just like those because he defied the armies of the living God. Saul decides to let him fight Goliath and tried to put his own armor on him. David was so small though that he could not even walk with all the armor Saul had put on him. David then took the armor off and went and found five smooth stones. Goliath then came out and saw that David was the one who decided to fight him. He saw that David was young and small so he cursed David. David then says, "You come to me with a sword, with a spear, and with a javelin. But I come to you in the name of the Lord of hosts, the God of the armies of Israel, whom you have defied. This day the Lord will deliver you into my hand, and I will strike you and take your head from you. And this day I will give the carcasses of the camp of the Philistines to the birds of the air and the wild beasts of the earth, that all the earth may know that there is a God in Israel." Then Goliath began to run toward David and David did not hesitate but ran straight toward him and took one of the stones he had and he slung it with his slingshot at Goliath. The Bible says that it sank deeply into his head. Then David took Goliath's own sword from him and cut his head off. Saul was fearful of Goliath and tried to have David wear his armor. David was not used to armor though. David knew that all he needed was the imputed power from God. The righteousness that God gave him. He had killed a lion and a bear before by that power and he saw Goliath as being the same as those. He also took five stones, not because he thought that he might miss, but because he knew that Goliath had four brothers and he planned that he would kill all four of them if they came out. He walked in the imputed power and righteousness of God. The first mention of David is when Samuel is talking to Saul about how the kingdom was going to be taken away from him and given to someone else. Samuel said that God had found another man after His own heart. That is who David was. His heart was directly connected to God's heart. The breastplate is the piece of armor that mainly protects the heart. The devil schemes to try to separate our heart from God. Our heart is separated from God when we walk in unrighteousness. We will always sin but we can ask for the forgiveness of God and have Christ's righteousness imputed to us. We do not need to walk in unrighteousness but walk in the righteousness that God has clothed us with. That is what David did and it will keep our heart connected to God's.

CHAPTER 7

Feet Shod with the Gospel of Peace

This chapter is going to focus on Ephesians 6:15 which says, "And having shod your feet with the preparation of the gospel of peace." The word shod means to actually bind something. This means that we must bind the gospel of peace on our feet to where it will not come off unless we willingly untie it. Having your feet shod with the gospel of peace is for the purpose of having peace and victory wherever we set our foot. It is also for us to deliver peace and victory wherever we step. Joshua 1:3 says, "Every place that the sole of your foot will tread upon I have given to you, as I said to Moses." This is about when Joshua took over leading the Israelites after Moses died. Joshua was appointed by God to lead them into the Promised Land. God said that wherever their feet step, He had already given it over to them. They already had victory over all the other inhabitants of the land because God had given it to them and was fighting for them. Now that we have Jesus living in us, we are able to have victory wherever we step. We are also able to spread peace over the land that we step on. We have victory over the devil where we step and because of that victory we are proclaiming peace in the areas that we walk.

The shoes that the Roman soldiers would bind to their feet had nails sticking out of the bottom of them because they usually traveled on very tough terrain. These nails would help to give traction to the ground so that they would not fall and be sure-footed during battle. If we have this then we are able to crush the enemy underneath our feet. Romans 16:19-20 says, "For your obedience has become known to all. Therefore I am glad on your behalf; but I want you to be wise in what is good and simple concerning evil. And the God of peace will crush Satan under your feet shortly. The grace of our Lord Jesus Christ be with you. Amen." Our God is a God of peace. The gospel that we have is full of peace and grace. If we have the gospel then we can live in and proclaim peace because we know that our enemy is defeated and that the Lord is going to crush Satan under our feet.

There are three points about binding your feet with the gospel of peace that I want to discuss. The first point is the preparation of binding our feet with the gospel of peace. We need to start every day by putting on the gospel of peace so that we can have victory throughout the rest of the day. Peace means to join with and to live in harmony with others. We must be joined with God. There are many ways that we can be joined with God and the first is best to do when you wake up. Read the Word of God everyday. As Christians we must know what the Bible says about us and what it tells us about God. The Bible is our basic instruction book that will help set us up for victory against the devil. We must be reading it everyday so that we are learning from it. Now this is not something that we do just to check off our list so we can continue on with the rest of our day, but we must be focused when we read it and looking for what God wants to tell us through reading it that day. I also do believe that it is best to do at the beginning of the day. It can be hard to stay focused because you can be tired, but if that is a problem, then make sure you have time to wake up enough or take a shower first to wake yourself up. Always make sure that you give yourself enough time to read the Bible in the morning. I had a time where I would get up at five because I started working at six.

If I got up that early, then I was guaranteed to have at least a half hour to read my Bible and pray to God for that day. This is the first way to join yourself to God every day.

The second way we can join ourselves with God is by memorizing the Word. It is essential to read the Word of God but we are also called to have the Word of God written on our hearts. Deuteronomy 11:18 says, "Therefore you shall lay up these words of mine in your heart and in your soul, and bind them as a sign on your hand, and they shall be as frontlets between your eyes." This is when God gave the Israelites the Law and He told them to bind it to themselves. Now we have the gospel that makes us able to fulfill the law and because of that we must know the Word of God by heart. We need to be able to pull Scripture out so that we can refute the lies that the devil is telling us and show that we are joined to God. One great way to do this is to just pick a verse or passage of Scripture and throughout the day read it over and over again. Then start to just recite it to yourself and not just say it but also concentrate on its meaning. By doing this it will become ingrained in your head and the meaning of the Scripture can also become enhanced because you have dwelt on it for the entire day. This is the second way to join ourselves with God.

The third way to join ourselves to God is through prayer. We must be in communion with God and prayer is basically just us talking to God and giving Him the chance to speak back to us. Prayer is our time to thank God for all that He has done for us and ask Him to bless us in areas of our life. It is also a time to bring our worries and request things for God to do. 1 Peter 5:7 says, "Casting all your care upon Him, for He cares for you." God cares about us and wants to know what is happening in our life. Truly God knows everything, so He does not need us to talk to Him but it is a necessity for us to have a relationship with Him. Speaking to God in prayer is a part of that relationship. Prayer is also not just for before you eat or go to bed, but it can continue throughout the day. I constantly pray to God for different things throughout the day. Certain things come up in my life and I just go straight to God in prayer and ask Him for His help in the certain area I am dealing with at the time. Praying does not have to be two hours set aside just to talk to God, but it can simply be two minutes in between classes or work related tasks. It helps us grow our relationship and lets God lead us in what He wants us to do. This is the third way to bind ourselves to God.

The fourth way to join yourself to God is to spend time worshiping Him. I play guitar and many times I just go in my room and play worship songs and sing to God. This is just one way that I worship God but there are countless ways to worship Him. It does not have to be through music. You can worship God through speaking and even just by enjoying His creation. Worshiping God is simply showing Him that He is worthy of all that we have. Find how you do that in your life and then continue to do it as an act of worship. Remember that the only thing the devil wants is for you to not worship God. As long as you are not worshiping Him then he is winning. This is the fourth way to bind ourselves to God.

The fifth way to bind ourselves to God is to listen to sermons. One thing that greatly helps us is to have a good understanding of the Bible. Sermons or podcasts are a great way to hear from pastors what the Bible is saying in certain areas. We can read the Bible and study it ourselves, but it does also help at times to learn from others who have studied it. You can also read commentaries of the Bible. One thing I do is that I have an app on my phone where I can download sermon podcasts and listen to them through my phone. I have listened to many different pastors whom I admire through this and have learned many things about the Bible through this asset. Church is a necessity and you do get sermons from going there, but if you want more, then these are great ways to be able to learn more from others. This is the fifth way to bind ourselves to God.

The sixth way to bind ourselves to God is through fellowship with other believers and accountability. We are to live in community with other believers. This helps edify us because we can learn from anyone who is in a relationship with God. We should be able to discuss God with people and see what He has revealed to them in their life. Accountability is a great way to do this. Accountability is when you have someone (of the same sex) that knows you very well that you can go to with struggles you have. It is not only for struggles, but just for prayer in areas of you life and to help build each other up. You can edify, encourage, pray for, and sometimes even confront them on things. Having accountability helps us in our fight against the devil because it is like having another warrior fighting alongside you. This is the sixth way that we are able to bind ourselves to God.

The final way we can bind ourselves to God is to acknowledge Him in the small areas. It is very easy for us to acknowledge and see God in the large areas of our life, but it can be hard for us to focus on Him being in the small areas of our life. We should be able to look at our whole life and see all that God has done for us. A quote from Mark Driscoll I heard once says, "Never question the providence of God, assume it." Providence does not mean that he will provide you with everything you want but that everything will work together for your good. Romans 8:28 says, "For we know that all things work together for good to those who love God, to those who are called according to His purpose." If we truly love God and we know that He has a purpose for us then we can assume that everything will work for our good. If you truly grasp this then you should be able to look back on your life and see that God had His hand in everything good that happened to you. Do not believe that it is just a coincidence, but acknowledge that it is God and give Him the glory for it. This is the final way to bind yourself to God.

The second point I want to discuss is that the gospel of peace is our protection. It keeps us from doing the wrong things or things that will eventually harm us. Romans 13:14 says, "But put on the Lord Jesus Christ, and make no provision for the flesh, to fulfill its lusts." By putting on the gospel of peace we are not letting the flesh be able to fulfill its desire. Instead we are allowing Christ to work through us and bring victory. The gospel of peace should be the guiding compass in every decision of our life because it will keep us from falling into the lust of the flesh. If we fulfill the desires of our flesh then we are surrendering ourselves to Satan. 1 Samuel 2:9 says, "He will guard the feet of

His saints, but the wicked shall be silent in darkness. For by strength no man shall prevail." It is not through our strength or anything we do on our own that we prevail over the lust of our flesh. It is only because God protects us from it. We all have evil desires, but we do not need to indulge in them because we have the power of Christ.

The third point I want to discuss is the purpose of binding our feet with the gospel of peace. As a believer, our purpose is to be a minister of the gospel of peace. Romans 10:15 says, "And how shall they preach unless they are sent? As it is written, 'How beautiful are the feet of those who preach the gospel of peace. Who bring glad tidings to the poor.'" The only way that we will be able to minister peace is if we are joined to God. He is the only one that gives us the ability to preach and lead others to Him. When you become a believer, God gives you the duty to go and disciple others. Matthew 28:19 says, "Go therefore and make disciples of all nations, baptizing them in the name of the Father, Son, and Holy Spirit." This is known as the Great Commission. This is what Jesus told his disciples to do the last time He saw them. This is a command to all believers that we are expected to do. We must be joined with God so that we have peace to minister with. Everywhere we step we are to be a minister of peace and to do that we must bind the gospel of peace to our feet.

CHAPTER 8

Shield of Faith

This chapter is going to focus on the next piece of the armor of God, which is the shield of faith. Ephesians 6:16 says, "Above all, taking the shield of faith with which you will be able to quench all the fiery darts of the wicked one." The main point of this chapter is that when I pick up my faith, I then access God's grace. We must know that the devil has a weapon formed against each one of us. There is not one all powerful weapon that the devil uses against all of us. He actually has a specific weapon that he uses against us. He finds our main weaknesses and then tempts us in those areas. When we pick up our faith we are able to have God protect us from that weapon. Isaiah 54:17 says, "No weapon formed against you shall prosper, and every tongue which rises against you in judgment you shall condemn. This is the heritage of the servants of the Lord, and their righteousness is from Me." When we are saved and pick up our faith God will destroy the weapon that Satan has formed against you. Faith is simply trusting in God's faithfulness. We can hold on to the promises that God has given us because He is faithful. He promises to work everything out to the good of those who love Him and are called according to His purpose so we can put faith into that promise. This is my favorite definition of faith. Faith is acting like it is so, when it is not so, that it may be so, just because God says so. Faith is the only way that we are justified. Romans 5:1-2 says, Therefore, having been justified by faith, we have peace with God through our Lord Jesus Christ, through whom we also have access by faith into this grace in which we stand, and rejoice in hope of the glory of God." We are justified by our faith in Christ alone. Because of that we are also able to access the grace that God has given us. The Bible specifically calls us to live and walk by our faith. Hebrews 10:38 says, "Now the just shall live by faith; but if anyone draws back, My soul has no pleasure in him". Colossians 2:6-7 says, "As you therefore have received Christ Jesus the Lord, so walk in Him, rooted and built up in Him and established in the faith, as you have been taught, abounding in it with thanksgiving."

We are established in Christ by our faith in Him. Our faith is the only way that we can be of and in Christ.

A Roman shield is made of wood and wrapped in leather. The Hebrew word for shield used in the Bible actually means door. This shield that they carried was not a small circular piece of wood but was an oblong four-cornered shield that was about as big as a regular door. It was made to cover almost the entire body. It was basically the riot shield of that day. Riot shields are also about as big as a door and the only difference is that they have a small window to see through and are completely bullet-proof. The shields were to protect the soldiers from being shot by arrows which is why it was wrapped in leather. An arrow would go through wood fairly easily but it is much harder for it to go through leather.

The Bible says that Jesus is our shield and door to God many times. John 10:7-11 says, Then Jesus said to them again, "Most assuredly I say to you. I am the door of the sheep. All whoever came before me were thieves and robbers, but the sheep did not hear them. I am the door, if anyone enters by Me, he will be saved, and will go in and out and find pasture. The thief does not come except to steal, to kill, and to destroy. I have come that they may have life, and that they may have it more abundantly. I am the good shepherd. The good shepherd lays down His life for the sheep." Jesus is willing to lay His life down for us to protect us and has laid His life down for us so that we will not go to hell. He is our shield and keeps us alive. Psalm 28:7 says, "The Lord is my strength and my shield; my heart trusted in Him, and I am helped; therefore my heart greatly rejoices, and with my song I will praise Him." Psalm 3:3 says, "But You, O Lord, are a shield for me; my glory and the One who lifts up my head." Jesus is our shield and strength against what the devil aims at us.

As I said earlier, the shield was to stop arrows but it would not protect anyone from flaming arrows. Flaming arrows were usually only aimed at the shield to dismantle the soldier so that he could easily be hit. Ephesians 6:16 says that the shield is able to quench all the fiery arrows of the evil one. The Roman soldiers would protect themselves from the flaming arrows by soaking the leather that they wrapped around their shield in water. This would make it extremely hard for the shield to catch on fire. As Christians we need to soak ourselves in faith in order to not be dismantled by the devil.

Now I want to discuss four ways that we are able to go deeper in the faith. The first is to ask for a double portion of the Spirit. 2 Kings 2:9 says, "And so it was, when they had crossed over, that Elijah said to Elisha,

"Ask! What may I do for you before I am taken away from you?" Elisha said, "Please let a double portion of your spirit be upon me." The story leading up to this verse is that Elijah was one of the greatest prophets of the Old Testament. He did many great things and even performed some miracles. Elisha was a man that was basically taught and mentored by Elijah. At the time when Elijah was about to be taken up to heaven, he asked what the last thing was he could do for Elisha. Elisha asked to have a double portion of his spirit as this verse says. Elijah then said that if Elisha sees him when he is taken away, then he will be given a double portion of his spirit. Elisha then watched as a chariot of fire came and separated him from Elijah and he saw Elijah go up to heaven in a whirlwind. Because of this Elisha was given a double portion of Elijah's spirit. Elisha did exactly double as many miracles as Elijah had done. We are able to walk in the power of the spirit when we ask God to fill us daily. Every day we should ask God to give us a double portion of His spirit so we are able to face anything that happens that day. Also Elisha saw that Elijah was always under great opposition. He wanted to have a double portion of his spirit so that he would be able to withstand the opposition that came his way. We need to be able to stand against any opposition that comes are way and having a double portion of the spirit is able to help us do that. The spirit gives us everything we need to be able to withstand the attacks of the enemy.

The second way to go deeper in our faith is to become a person of prayer. Ephesians 6:18 says, "Praying always with all prayer and supplication in the Spirit, being watchful to this end with all perseverance and supplication for all the saints." Some people believe that when it says to be praying with prayer and supplication in the Spirit, it means to pray in tongues. The gift of tongues is a great gift when used correctly, but that is not what this verse means. It means that we are praying through the spirit that God has given us. It also says that we must always pray through the spirit. Our prayers should always come from our spirit and not just our own desires. Our spirit is what tells us the desires God has for our life. James 5:15-16 says, "And the prayer of faith will save the sick, and the Lord will raise him up. And if he has committed sins, he shall be forgiven. Confess your trespasses to one another, and pray for one another that you may be healed. The effective, fervent prayer of a righteous man avails much." This verse says that if we pray in faith then it will heal the sick. We are able to do all the miracles that Jesus performed if we pray in complete faith that it will happen. Faith is also the only way that our sins will be forgiven. This verse also talks about accountability. It tells us to confess our sins to each other. We should have a person that we can go to that knows us and loves us very much. We can confess our sins to them and instead of judging us they should pray with and for us. By this we are able to be healed. The prayer of a righteous man avails much. By our faith in Jesus Christ we are made righteous by his death on the cross. We should be people of prayer and pray through the spirit for anything that we need every day.

The third way to go deeper in our faith is to become a student of God's Word. Colossians 3:16 says, "Let the word of Christ dwell in you richly in all wisdom, teaching and admonishing one another in all psalms and hymns and spiritual songs, singing with grace in your hearts to the Lord." We should know the word of God. It says that it should dwell in our hearts richly. It should be basically pouring out of our hearts because of how richly it is in us. This verse also says to teach others. No matter who you are God has revealed a specific thing to you that he wants you to teach others. Personally, God has taught me many things which I have then written in my books to teach to others so that they have part of the knowledge that God has given to me. We are to disciple others, and teaching them about God is the biggest part of the discipleship process. It says that we can also do this in spiritual songs. I listen to many different bands, but they are all Christian except for two. By listening to many different Christian musical artists I have been amazed at times how most of them are able to teach and give great truths about the Bible and God through their music. Some bands have extremely deep lyrics in their songs and some don't but they still can edify us. We do not need to listen to Christian music only but I do encourage that it should be something that we listen to because it is giving us the truth of God instead of what the secular world is trying to throw at us. Finally, this verse says to have hearts of grace. It is impossible to give good truth to others if we do not have grace toward them and only judgment. We must be able to give grace freely as Christ did. 1 John 2:14 says, "I have written to you, Father, because you have known Him who is from the beginning. I write to you, young men, because you are strong, and the word of God abides in you, and you have overcome the wicked one." Him who is from the beginning is Jesus. John 1:1 says, "In the beginning was the Word, and the Word was with God, and the Word was God." Jesus is the Word. It says that he is writing to the young men because they are strong. The word of God abides in them and because of that they have overcome the wicked one who is Satan. When we have God's word abiding in us, we are able to overcome the devil and stand up against his attacks.

The fourth is to commit yourself to a strong community of faith. Ecclesiastes 4:9-12 says, "Two are better than one, because they have a good reward for their labor. For if they fall, one will lift up his companion. But woe to him who is alone when he falls. For he has no one to help him up. Again if two lie down together, they will keep warm; but how can one be warm alone. Though one may be overpowered by another, two can withstand him. And a threefold cord is not quickly broken." It is not enough for us to just go to church. We need to be connecting with the people there. As this verse says, if there are two then they can withstand anything that cannot be withstood alone. We are called to help a brother or sister in Christ up when they fall. When we fall church is a great place to find people that are going through the same thing and there are others that will be able to pull you back up. By yourself it is much easier to be overcome by the devil; but as it says a cord of three strands is very hard to break. Being in a community can greatly help us when battling against the devil.

I want to end this chapter with the verse 1 John 5:4. "For whatever is born of God overcomes the world. And this is the victory that has overcome the world, our faith."

CHAPTER 9

Helmet of Salvation

In this chapter we will focus on what is presented in the first half of Ephesians 6:17. "And take the helmet of Salvation." 1 Peter 5:8 says, "Be sober, be vigilant; because your adversary the devil walks around like a roaring lion, seeking whom he may devour." One thing that Satan wants to do is occupy your mind. Occupy means that he seizes or controls your mind. This verse tells us to be sober and vigilant. If our mind is fortified then it may not be occupied by the devil. That is why it also says that the devil is seeking whom he may devour. He knows that he cannot devour anyone but he is desperately seeking those whose minds are not fortified because he will be able to easily occupy them. The thing that is occupying Satan's mind is to occupy other's minds. Job 1:6-8 shows the devil doing this. It says, "Now there was a day when the sons of God came to present themselves before the Lord, and Satan also came among them. And the Lord said to Satan, "From where do you come?" So Satan answered the Lord and said, "From going to and fro from the earth, and walking back and forth on it." Then the Lord said to Satan, "Have you considered my servant Job, that there is none like him on the earth, a blameless and upright man, one who fears God and shuns evil?" Satan says that he has come from going all over the earth and he is seeking someone to devour. He walks with great eagerness to find those that are not strong enough to stand against his attacks. Revelation 12:12 says, "Therefore rejoice, O heavens, and you who dwell in them! Woe to the inhabitants of the earth and the sea! For the devil has come down to you, having great wrath, because he knows that he has a short time." The devil knows that Christ is getting ready to come back. Ever since Christ rose to heaven we have been in the end times, we just do not know if we are in the last days. The devil has no idea when Christ is going to come back but he knows that He will, and the time is short. This is why he walks with such eagerness. He must find the ones that he may devour soon before Christ comes back and sends him to Hades. Revelation 1:17-18 says, "And when I saw Him, I fell at His feet as dead. But He laid His right hand on me, saying to me, "Do not be afraid; I am the First and the Last. I am He who lives, and was dead, and behold, I am alive forevermore. Amen. And I have the keys to death and Hades." The devil used to have the keys to death and Hades but when Christ died He went and took the keys from him and rose victoriously over the devil. Now God is the ruler over Hades and it is for the devil and those who follow him.

Peter uses his description of the devil being a lion very wisely because he knew that the Israelites would understand it. At this time there were many lions in Israel and there are three characteristics of lions that are very similar to the devil. The first is that lions are nocturnal. Lions always do their best work at night. The devil likes to work in the darkness. Romans 13:12-14 says, "The night is far spent, the day is at hand. Therefore let us cast of the works of darkness, and let us put on the armor of light. Let us walk properly, as in the day, not in revelry and drunkenness, not in lewdness and lust, not in strife and envy. But put on the Lord Jesus Christ, and make no provision for the flesh, to fulfill its lusts." The things that are listed in this verse usually happen at night or near nighttime. Revelry means a boisterous celebration. Also many people will only get drunk at night and while in this state their mind is not fortified and it is easy for the devil to make them do stupid things. Lewdness means that you are obscene or indecent. As Christians we should not act in this way because we are supposed to represent Christ. Also nighttime seems to be an opportune time to lust. Many masturbate at night because it is when they will most likely not have anyone find them and you must be lusting to masturbate. Night is also when most people will dwell on the strife they have with others or how much they envy another person. These are all wrong things to do and they happen mostly at night. Instead of doing these we are told to put on the armor of light and make no provision for the flesh. The flesh will want to do most of these things but we should not let ourselves fall into them. Ephesians 5:11-13 says, "And have no fellowship with the unfruitful works of the darkness, but rather expose them. For it is shameful to even speak of those things which are done by them in secret. But all things that are exposed are made manifest by the light, for whatever makes manifest is light." We should not have fellowship with those that do the works of the darkness, however, we should try to reach them and show them love, but do not join them in these practices. Also the light exposes them for what they really are. If we are guided by the light, then we will know that these all lead to darkness. Sadly, there are many Christians that engage in this behavior and are willingly living in the darkness when they know that they should not. If you are willingly in darkness, then you should assume that your mind will be occupied by the devil. When we come into the darkness it is easy for Satan to devour us.

The second characteristic of a lion is that it cannot see small things apart from large things. For example, I went on a mission trip to South Africa a few years ago and got to go on a safari where we saw lions. The man driving the truck said that we must stay in the truck otherwise the lions would most likely try to attack us. At first this did not make sense because I thought they might attack us even if we were in the truck. The reason they don't is because when a person is in a truck they do not see the person. All the lion sees is a truck. They only see something that is bigger and stronger than they are so they will stay away from it. When a person comes out of the truck then they are able to be seen by the lion and the lion knows it is stronger than a human. Because of this they would only try to attack you if you are outside of the truck. It is the same with the devil. The devil will not try to overtake you if you are in something that is greater than him. This is why we need to be in Christ. Philippians 4:7 says, "And the peace of God, which surpasses all understanding, will guard your hearts and minds through Christ Jesus. If we are in Christ then he will protect our hearts and minds. In Christ basically means that we are saved. That is why it is the helmet of salvation. Our salvation will guard and protect our mind. The phrase in Christ actually appears 87 times in the New Testament and always refers to being saved. When we are in Christ the devil only sees that we are guarded by Him and because Christ has already defeated the devil he knows that Jesus is stronger and greater than him. Because of this he will not try to devour you.

The third characteristic is that lions are territorial. The lions do not want any other animals to be in their area. If an animal comes in their territory, they will run it off by intimidation. All animals are first afraid of people. They are fearful of us until they see that we are fearful. It is when they see the weakness in us of being fearful of them that they will attack us. If you turn they will attack but if you stand firm they will back down. Satan wants to be like the Most High. He never says that He wants to be higher that God because he knows he cannot be, so he just wants to be like Him. We must know that God is the highest and there can be no one higher. Colossians 1:13 says, "He has delivered us from the power of darkness and conveyed us into the kingdom of the Son of His love. Satan lost his territory when we were saved by Jesus. Until we are saved we are in the kingdom of darkness and are occupied by Satan.

We do the things of darkness and have no forgiveness for them because we have not had Jesus forgive us for our sins which we committed. Because of this we are a servant of the darkness but when we surrender to Jesus we become a servant of Him and He takes us from the darkness which was Satan's territory. That is not the only territory that Satan has lost. The first territory that he lost was his place in heaven. Before he was the enemy of God, he was the worshipper of God. His job was to usher all worship and praise to Him. Then he said in his heart that he wanted to be exalted as God and he held back some of the worship for himself. Because of this God cast him out of heaven. Revelation 12:9 says, "So the great dragon was cast out, that serpent of old, called the devil and Satan, who deceives the whole world; he was cast to the earth and his angels were cast out with him." He lost his territory in heaven but then had territory in people's minds. It was bad for him to just lose his first territory but it is terrible when he looses the only other territory he has. It must drive him crazy. Because of this he tries to go after the minds of the believers and draw them back into the dark. As lions roar, the devil also roars lies at believers. He will accuse us and condemn us. He will bring up sins of our past and say that God will not accept anyone who has done this. Obviously you cannot be saved. He also brings up what we have done after we were saved and make us doubt our salvation by saying that anyone who is truly saved would never sin this much or in this way again. This shows that you were never really saved. Many people come to believe this and it makes them scared for their life. The devils main objective at telling us these lies is that he wants to scare us and scatter us. When we become scared we go back to what is familiar to us. The thing that is familiar to us is the darkness which Jesus had pulled you out of. Instead we need to not be scared by these accusations and know that God is our salvation. Isaiah 12:2 says, Behold, God is my salvation, I will trust and not be afraid; For YAH, the Lord, is my strength and song; He also has become my salvation."

The book of Romans gives us a way to stand against the devil when he does this. The first eleven chapters of Romans focuses on everything we need to know. Chapter twelve tells us what to do in view of what we know. Romans 12:1-2 says, "I beseech you, therefore brethren, by the mercies of God, that you present your bodies a living sacrifice, holy, acceptable to God, which is your reasonable service. And do not be conformed to this world, but be transformed by the renewing of your mind, that you may prove what is that good and acceptable and pure will of God." This verse tells us that we must renew our mind and if we renew our mind then we will be transformed. There are four ways to renew our mind. The first is to memorize God's Word. If we memorize the Word of God then it will be stuck in our mind and we are able to pull it out whenever we need to refute the devil. We should first of all memorize and know what the Word says about us now that we are God's. God calls us his children and says that he sees us blameless and pure like his son. We should know this and have it renew our mind to understand that there is no more sin in us when we surrender our lives to Christ.

The second way to renew our mind is to meditate on God's word. We should first know these scriptures and then meditate on them throughout the day. Think about what it means that you are now a child of God and that He loves you more than anything else He created. Meditate on what it means to have been made clean and that you are pure because Jesus died for all your sins. Let the understanding and revelation of these renew your mind.

The third thing is to destroy the arguments and accusations. Now that you know the truth of what the Bible says about you and the way God sees you, then you can prove the lies from the devil wrong. You can be sure that God does not care what sins you have committed and that you can always receive forgiveness for them. You can also be sure that even if you did sin while you were saved, those sins are wiped clean from you too. God does not see any sin you have done or will ever do. By this you can stand strong in your salvation.

Lastly, you must take every thought captive. Analyze your thoughts and see if they are lies from the devil or truth from God's Word. This will help you to only have your mind be occupied by the things of God. I want to end with the verses so that you know that God is there to help you with anything that might be hard to handle in your mind. I Peter 5:6-7, "Therefore humble yourselves under the mighty hand of God, that He may exalt you in due time, casting all your care upon Him, for He cares for you."

CHAPTER 10

Sword of the Spirit

This chapter will conclude the armor of God with the second half of Ephesians 6:17. "And take the sword of the Spirit, which is the word of God." One thing that we must understand is that whatever happens in the spirit realm influences the physical. That is why it is the sword of the Spirit. Every other piece of armor is about different things that we can do with God. This one is something only God can do. We can pray to God and ask things to happen in the spiritual realm, but overall it is all done by God. We still need to do a lot with this piece of armor but we must know that it is only by us following God that He will side with us and do things in the spiritual realm.

The main point of this chapter is that stronger is always better than strong. I know this feels like a "duh" statement, but it is the overlying theme of this entire chapter so if you know nothing else after this chapter is over, at least know that. We need to be strong but always continue to get stronger. It is like when you go to work out at a gym. You can go for a couple of days and start building muscle. You will begin to get stronger but if you stop for a little bit, everything you gained will just go away. Then you need to start over from exactly where you were before you started. I have done this many times and it is always extremely frustrating for me that I let myself stop instead of keeping myself going. This is the same way. We can be strong and get better at fighting the spiritual war, but then relax because we believe that we have overcome enough and then the devil will hit us hardest and we will usually fall miserably. I have friends that have battled with pornography and masturbation and who have said that they have overcome it. Then within the next year they will fall into it or do worse things than it. One person I know actually ended up having sex with a woman outside of marriage and it was because he became relaxed and did not fortify himself. He thought that he could resist anything that would come after him. In the Sermon on the Mount Christ said in Matthew 5:29, "If your right eye causes you to sin, pluck it out and cast it from you, for it is more profitable for you that one of your members perish, than your whole body to be cast into hell." This verse can cause problems for some people because they cannot believe that Jesus would want us to self-mutilate ourselves. The truth of what he is saying is that if you know something might cause you to enter into sin then don't do it. For example, if you know that making out with you girlfriend or boyfriend will lead you either into sin or close to doing a sinful act, then you should not do it. It also says in this verse your right eye. Most people are right eye dominant so this means taking something away from you that is very useful. This is like a computer being extremely helpful but if it is easy for you to sin by doing certain good things on the computer, then you should not have one or find ways to make it impossible for you to be able to sin while on it. This is a way to make yourself stronger. We need to always continue to fortify ourselves while fighting this battle.

Roman soldiers would always carry two different swords with them. They had their regular sword and also an eighteen inch dagger. The Greek word used for sword in this verse is "machaira", which means a small sword use for skillfully cutting flesh. This verse is talking about the dagger. It does not mean you have this large and long sword that keeps the enemy at least an arm's length away, but a dagger that would be used for extremely close range battle. Also this is the only offensive part of the armor of God. Every other piece was to help us stand our ground and defend us from the enemy's attacks. This one is meant to take ground. It would take a lot of skill to effectively take ground with an eighteen inch dagger. It would take a lot of skill to fight someone with just an eighteen inch dagger, and yet this is the piece that Paul says we use to offensively fight the enemy. This means that we need to make ourselves extremely skillful at wielding it and it will take a lot of continuous work. It is not something that we can start to get good at and then stop working on it and still be good. We must always be working on it and we can always get better.

2 Corinthians 10:3-4 says, "For though we walk in the flesh, we do not war according to the flesh. For the weapons of our warfare are not carnal but mighty in God for pulling down strongholds." We are in the flesh on this earth and are told to war in the Spirit realm. The only way that we are able to do this is by God. As I said earlier, He is the only one that can affect the Spirit world for us. We must be mighty in God and have Him fight for us. The way that we get Him to fight for us is by following His commands. I am not saying that we can never sin again because we will fail, but we need to live in a way that pleases Him and brings

Him glory. Ephesians 6:17 says that the sword of the spirit is the word of God. There are three words used in the Bible for the word of God. The first is "kathab" which is the scriptures. This is what is written in the Bible. The second word is "logos". This one means the understanding of the scriptures. This is being able to pull out from the scriptures what is truly meant by it and find ways to apply it to our lives. The third is "rhema". This means taking what the scriptures say and understanding them and applying them. It is the acting out of following the Bible. This is the word that is used in this verse. To wield the sword of the Spirit we must act out what the Bible has told us to do. When we do that, God gives us the power and strength to pull down the strongholds that are in our life. This is the only way that we can take ground and be able to start defeating the devil in the spiritual war.

To show what I mean by following what God commands, I will use the story of Asa. The story of Asa is recorded in 2 Chronicles 14. Verse 1 says, "So Abijah rested with his fathers, and they buried him in the City of David. Then Asa his son reigned in his place. In his days the land was quiet for ten years." Abijah did evil in the sight of the Lord. He and his mother put up two sex gods and worshiped them. One was a god that had very large male genitals. Actually many people of that time believed that the Gods had huge sex organs so they would put up large carved images of the male genitalia and it would be an idol that they worshiped. The other god that they put up was a goddess that stood for fertility and she was covered in breasts all over her body. Asa's father and grandmother served and worshiped these two gods before he became king. Verse 2-5 says, "Asa did what was good in the eyes of the Lord and his God, for he removed the altars of the foreign gods and high places, and broke down the sacred pillars and cut down the wooden images. He commanded Judah to seek the Lord God of their fathers, and to observe the law and the commandment. He also removed the high places and the incense altars from all the cities of Judah, and the kingdom was quiet under him." Asa did not do as his father did. He actually walked in his authority. Much of the evil that Abijah did was because he was influence by his mother. He followed what she wanted instead of taking full authority and leading the kingdom in the right ways. Asa took full authority and followed God. He destroyed all the foreign gods that had invaded Israel by the countries surrounding them. He broke and destroyed all the sacred pillars and cut down all the wooden images of the other gods that his father worshiped. He commanded the kingdom turn back to God and seek Him and observe His commandment to serve Him only. He removed the high places and incense altars where the people would sacrifice things to these other gods. He also had his grandmother thrown out of the palace. It is hard for me to even imagine having to throw my grandmother out of my own house, but he threw her out of the entire city. He wanted to follow God so much that he had her removed from where she had been for years. Because of all this the kingdom was quiet under him for ten years. This means that there was no war for ten years while he was king. Verses 6-8 say, "And he built fortified cities in Judah, for the land had rest; he had no war in those years, because the Lord had given him rest. Therefore he said to Judah, "Let us build these cities and make walls around them, and towers, gates, and bars, while the land is yet before us, because we have sought the Lord our God; we have sought Him and He has given us rest on every side." So they built and prospered. And Asa had an army of three hundred thousand from Judah who carried shields and spears, and from Benjamin two hundred and eighty thousand men who carried shields and drew bows; all these were mighty men of valor." While the kingdom had rest and there was no war, Asa fortified the cities of Judah. He built up the defenses in the city to make them stronger and harder for other countries to come and seize them. He told Judah that they would do this because they had sought the Lord and He had given them rest on every side. He did not see the blessing of no war as a time to relax, but as a time to build up the cities and his army. It says they built and prospered and then it tells us of the army that he had from Judah and Benjamin. He did not waste the time he had but used it to make everything stronger. Verses 9-13 say, "Then Zerah the Ethiopian came out against them with an army of a million men and three hundred chariots, and he came to Mareshah. So Asa went out against him and they set troops in battle array in the Valley of Zephathah at Mareshah. And Asa cried out to the Lord his God, and said, "Lord, it is nothing for You to help, whether with many or those who have no power, help us, O Lord our God, for we rest on You, and in Your name we go against this multitude. O Lord, you are our God; and do not let man prevail against You!" So the Lord struck the Ethiopians before Asa and Judah, and the Ethiopians fled. And Asa and the people who were with him pursued them to Gerar. So the Ethiopians were overthrown, and they could not recover, for they were broken before the Lord and His army. And they carried away very much spoil." After ten years of no war, the Ethiopians came out to war against Him. Before they began to fight Asa cried out to the Lord. He said that they rest on Him alone. He knew that the only way that they would win would be if God fought for them. He stepped out in complete faith that God would overcome the Ethiopians and have them destroyed before Israel. It says that the Lord then struck the Ethiopians and they fled before Asa and the army. Asa and the army chased after them and defeated them in such a way that they could not recover. If we call out to God to fight for us He will but we must also fight against them and destroy them completely. The Ethiopians had no way to be built back up after Israel overcame them. God does not want to have strongholds against us be built back up. God will fight for us and defeat them, but we must continue to act out and make it to where the strongholds can never be built up after they have been torn down. Do not just keep the enemy at bay but have our life be completely changed because he has no forces against us. Verse 14-15 says, "Then they defeated all the cities around Gerar, for the fear of the Lord came upon them; and they plundered all the cities, for there was exceedingly much spoil in them. They also attacked the livestock enclosures, and carried off sheep and camels in abundance, and returned to Jerusalem." They were then able to defeat all the other cities and took everything that they had. They would not allow any of the cities to be able to come against them. Asa followed the commands of the Lord and did great things for the nation. We need to be like this and apply what the word has said to us so that we can wield the sword of the Spirit and pull down the strongholds and have them never recover. That is how we win the war.

CHAPTER 11

Prayer

So far we have looked at where the war began and how we put on the armor of God and fight. Now we will discuss the single greatest thing we can do in this battle. It is named after the armor of God in Ephesians 6:18. "Praying always with all prayer and supplication in the Spirit, being watchful to this end with all perseverance and supplication for all the saints." Prayer is the most essential part of us being able to survive in Spiritual Warfare. Communication is the greatest essential key to any victory. Not long ago a movie called *Lone Survivor* came out about four Navy Seals who were sent to assassinate a certain Taliban leader. While they were near the town where the man was, they found a child and his grandfather. They had to choose to kill them both and carry on with the mission, or let them go and abort the mission. They decide to let them go and they headed back up the mountain from which they came. But they had a problem; they were not able to communicate to let anyone else know that they had aborted the mission and that they would soon be surrounded by Taliban that were going to try to kill them all. Because of this, three of the men died and only one man made it out alive. The communication was cut and the price of it was death. If our communication is cut, it will most likely lead to us being spiritually dead, which will end in us losing the spiritual war. Satan will try his hardest to cut our communication with God.

Communication is a two way street. There must be an effort on both sides to have true communication. Prayer is our communication with God so it is us talking to Him and in turn God talking to us. When Satan tries to sever our lines of communication, he will only come after us. This is because he cannot stop God. He has been defeated by him and has no power over what God does. Satan will try to stop us though and if he does, God would want to communicate with us but can't because we are choosing not to communicate with Him. As I said, there must be an effort on both sides for there to be communication. We can put on all the armor of God but it is in the end completely useless if we do not have prayer. The devil has been able to sever the lines of communication with so many mostly because we have the wrong view of what prayer is. The definition of prayer is to interact with the Lord by switching human wishes for divine wishes as He imparts faith and wisdom. A lot of times we pray just to have our wishes granted to us. That is not how prayer should be. Prayer should be us making our wishes known to God and then have God show us His true wishes for us and us understanding that they are better than our own. God sees differently than we do. He sees how everything will turn out so He knows what is best for us. When we pray God allows us to see from His viewpoint by giving us the wisdom and faith that He has everything working together for our own good.

There are three points about what prayer is not that I want to go through so that we can have a better understanding of what true prayer is and be able to use it to win the battle. The first point is that prayer is not about a religious requirement. Prayer is about a relational response. Many people approach prayer as something that we do so that we are good Christians. Jesus rebuked the Pharisees of doing this in Matthew 6:5. He says, "And when you pray, you shall not be like the hypocrites. For they love to pray standing in the synagogues and on the corners of the streets, that they may be seen by men. Assuredly, I say to you, they have their reward." The Pharisees would pray in front of many people to show how religious they were and not to communicate with God. You might not try to impress people but it is the same if you pray just because that is what Christians are supposed to do. It should always be the way that we connect with God. Most Christians usually pray before we eat, when we go to bed, at church, and before sporting events. Sometimes our most fervent prayers are during sporting events especially when our team is losing. I am not saying that we should not pray at these times, but that should not be the only times we pray. We should engage in a lifestyle of prayer where it is something that we do because we actually want to have relational communication with God and not just to be "good" Christians.

Also there are many that will pray in Jesus' name and in the same breath use His name in vain. This also happens most times during sporting events. Truly most cuss words do not bother me. Not even the "f" word bothers me as much as people using God's name in vain. Look at any other religion and you will never see them use their god's name in vain. No one ever hurts themselves and screams out "Buddha". It is only the name of the one true God that gets used as a cuss word. This can damage our prayers because His name is to be holy and this is making it unholy and makes us have no reverence for Him when we enter into prayer. All kinds of this talk should be cut out of our vocabulary. And yes even the phrase "oh my God" is using His name in vain. This gives no reverence to God and makes it unholy.

There are also a number of questions that people have about prayer. The three most common ones are: is there a certain amount; what do we say; and do we have a long enough list? I will try to answer these questions the best way I can right now. First, is there a certain amount of time that I should pray? Truly many Christian leaders will say that you must pray for at least two hours a day or some other amount of time. I will answer this with what Smith Wigglesworth said in an interview once. Smith Wigglesworth was a man that did some of the most amazing miracles ever. He raised numerous people from the grave. At one time he actually took a dead baby and literally punted it into a crowd of people and it landed in a woman's hands alive. He was once asked how long he prays. He said, "I never pray more than five to ten minutes." He then said, "but I never go more than five to ten minutes without praying." Basically there is no true amount of time that you should pray, but just pray to God throughout the day, when people ask you to, or when you need to because something comes up in your life. Also pray to God to thank him for things in your life that are going well. At times I just thank God for giving me the right way to handle a situation and that is my entire prayer.

Next, what should I say in prayer? This one I have for the most part already answered. When you pray, first address God with reverence. Then thank Him for everything He has done. After that just make your requests known to Him and ask Him to also give you His desires so that they are not merely human desires. This is how Jesus taught His disciples to pray. The Lord's Prayer is just the basic model prayer that we can follow as a guide of how we pray to God. It is found in Matthew 6:9-13.

Lastly, do I have a long enough list? Many people make a list of points that they want to pray for. Truly there are no length requirements for a prayer list. Mainly this is because lists change but I do encourage people to have a list because it can help us to know what we need to pray for instead of just mindlessly praying for random things. Just make sure that your prayer list has everything on it that you want and believe you should pray about.

The last thing on this point is that prayer does not have to be done in a holy or religious place. I have nothing against prayer rooms, but I know that some people get the wrong idea about them. Some people come to believe that the prayer room is this extremely holy place and if you go into it your prayers are for sure heard by God. We can treat them like the temple from the Old Testament. In the Old Testament people had to go to a temple to pray because there was no way for God to be with us everywhere. When Jesus died on the cross there was then a way for God to come and live inside of us. Because of this the temple now lives in us. 1 Corinthians 6:19 says, "Or do you not know that your body is the temple of the Holy Spirit whom is in you, whom you have from God, and you are not your own?" Because our body is the temple any place we go can be a holy place and there is no specific place that we must pray.

The second point is prayer is not your preferences, it is God's purposes. One of the largest hurdles for people is that if God hears our prayers why does He not answer them? First this thinking makes God out to look like some fairy or genie. Ask Him anything we want and He will automatically do it for us because He loves us. Truly He will deny us of some of our preferences because He loves us so much. Prayer should not be something we do to get what we want, but something we do so we can see if what we want is what God wants. Isaiah 55:8-9 says, "For My thoughts are not your thoughts, nor are My ways your ways," says the Lord. "For as the heavens are higher than the earth, so are My ways higher than your ways, and My thoughts than your thoughts." God sees and understands more than we ever will, so He knows not to answer certain things that we ask for. Also, we should trust God with everything by saying not my will but Yours be done. Luke 22:39-43 says, "Coming out, He (Jesus) went to the Mount of Olives, as He was accustomed, and His disciples also followed Him. When He came to the place, He said to them, "Pray that you may not enter into temptation." And He was withdrawn from them a stone's throw, and He knelt down and prayed, saying, "Father, if it is Your will, take this cup away from me; Nevertheless not my will, but Yours be done." Then an angel appeared to Him from heaven, strengthening Him." Jesus prayed this right before He was going to be seized by Romans and crucified. The cup He asked to pass from Him was the sin of all the earth, past and future. He asked if there was any other way to save humanity and there was none. So He willingly went to His death. If God would have answered what He wished for then there would be no redemption for the world and we would all go to hell. We should thank God that He does not always give us what we want when we ask for it in prayer. Also when we pray like this the ministry of the Lord will come to you and you will be strengthened to complete His purposes as Jesus was. The third point is prayer is not limited to where you are geographically but birthed out of where you are spiritually. A lot of times we believe that our prayers for some place can only make a difference if we are there. Or that our prayers would only make a difference for a certain situation if we were in that specific situation. We need to know that no matter what, we can always make a difference anywhere for anything by intercession. Intercession is going on someone's behalf and praying for God to help them or that area. Prayer is not only for our requests to be made known to God but for other's requests also.

The last thing that people usually want to know about prayer is how to deepen it. The truth is that there is not a tried and true way known to deepen a prayer life. The only way I know is the same way to deepen a friendship. You must first both decide to be friends and then put effort into getting to know each other and get into each other's lives. Basically the best way to start to deepen your prayer life is to just start praying and through the action of praying it will naturally develop. So do not wait, but start praying now and do not leave this essential element out of your life.

CHAPTER 12

Thrive

In this chapter we are going to discuss how to stay alive and thrive while fighting in Spiritual Warfare. There is a song by the band *Switchfoot* called Thrive. The lyrics say, "I feel like I travel but never arrive. I want to thrive, not just survive." If we really think about this it is very true. No one wants to just survive and stay alive in life. We want to actually do something that matters. We do not want to feel like we are just traveling through life without ever accomplishing anything. When we are thriving we know that we are accomplishing something great in this world or the Spiritual one. I am going to discuss three principles on how we can thrive in life while also fighting in the spiritual war.

The first principle is to be on guard at every moment. We need to be aware, awake, and watchful. We must always be ready for when the enemy attacks. Now it is usually different for every person when the enemy attacks, but there are four universal times that he will attack. The first is when you wake up. Satan will try to attack us when we wake up because we are still sleepy and will not be fully awake. Also it is a great time for him to attack because if he can hurt us at the very beginning of the day, then it will be easier to get us the rest of the day. He wants to mess up our day from the start. The best way to counteract this is to give God the first fruits of your day. This means that we need to get with Him at the beginning of our day and connect with Him. At one time I was the shift leader for a breakfast crew. This meant I was in charge of all the people that served breakfast at a cafeteria and would make sure that everything went well and was done correctly. Breakfast was usually served at seven, so I would always get there at six to set everything up and make the food. I would get up just in time to take a shower and head down there, which meant I would not get with God. When I realized that this was not good for me to do, I started to get up at five so that I had at least thirty minutes to spend in God's word and pray for the day. Sometimes we need to fight to make time for us to get alone with God. It helps keep us from being messed up from the beginning of the day.

The second time Satan will attack you is when going to bed. This is like we are when we wake up. We have been doing things all day long and are tired, so we are not always aware as we should be. The way to counteract this is to take every thought captive. The devil will put thoughts in your mind to tempt you but if you take every thought and examine to see if it is good or bad then you should be able to determine who it is from and to turn away from the ones from the devil. Flee from the temptation that he uses to try to make us sin.

The third time he attacks is when our mind is idle. The truth is that it is extremely hard to be aware all the time, so our mind can become idle and we cannot be on guard at all times. The way to counteract this is to ask God for the ability to continue to be aware and set your mind on Him in these times. God will strengthen you if you are doing this to keep from sinning, and if your mind is set on Him then you will rarely be drawn into following temptations.

The fourth main time Satan attacks is when we are traveling. I was at an internship for two years with Teen Mania Ministries. While there I was always surrounded with amazing godly people and everyone was growing closer to God and learning more about Him. It was like we were in a greenhouse, we grew so much in the Lord. When I would go home, all that changed. It was not that my family did not love God, but just that I was not in that greenhouse environment. My family absolutely loves and follows God, but I was just not used to being out of the greenhouse. Because of this it was an easier time for the devil to attack me. I would get hit very hard with many temptations. The only way I could counteract it was to remain on guard and ask for the power of God to guard my heart. We need His power when protecting ourselves during these times when we are most tempted.

Also during this first point I want to look at the three main tactics that the devil uses. Luke 4:1-13 tells us the story of when Jesus was tempted by the devil. It says, "Then Jesus being filled with the Holy Spirit, returned from the Jordan and was led by the Spirit into the wilderness, being tempted for forty days by the devil. And in those days He ate nothing, and afterward, when they ended, He was hungry. And the devil said to Him, "If you are the son of God, command this stone to become bread." But Jesus answered him saying, "It is written, man shall not live by bread alone, but by every word of God." Then the devil taking Him up to a high mountain, showed Him all the kingdoms of the world in a moment of time. And the devil said to Him, "All this authority I will give You, and their glory; for this has been delivered to me, and I give it to whomever I wish. Therefore, if You worship before me, all will be Yours." And Jesus answered and said to Him, "Get behind Me, Satan! For it is written, You shall worship the Lord your God and Him only you shall serve." Then he brought Him to Jerusalem, set Him on the pinnacle of the temple, and said to Him, "If You are the son of God, throw Yourself down from here. For it is written, He shall give His angels charge over You, to keep You, and, In their hands they shall bear You up, lest you dash Your foot against a stone." And Jesus answered and said to Him. "It has been said, You shall not tempt the Lord your God." Now when the devil had ended every temptation, he departed from Him until an opportune time." In this passage we see the three tactics the devil uses in these temptations. The first tactic is that the devil will always come when you are weak and where you are weak. He came to Jesus when He was extremely hungry and tempted Him to turn a stone into bread. The second tactic is that Satan will make you question your identity of who you are in the Lord. He said to Jesus, "If you are the Son of God." He tried to make Him question who He was so that He would prove it. The third tactic is that Satan will always try to pervert, distort, or discount who God is and His truths. Satan used Scripture about what God promises He will do in his third temptation. He tried to distort it and show that it was not true. I want you to notice one main thing in this passage, and that is that Jesus answered the devil's temptations by using Scripture. He even did that when the devil used Scripture. The best way to fight temptation is with Scripture. This is why we must memorize the Word of God. We must be ready with Scripture to combat every temptation that the devil throws at us. The last verse says that the devil departed until an opportune time. We must always be on guard because the second we aren't, the devil will see that it is an opportune time. This will help us to thrive because we are not falling into sin which means that we are being successful in the battle.

The second principle is to persevere in all situations. The Greek word for perseverance used in Ephesians 6:18 is "proskarteresis". It is derived from the Greek word Proskartero which has six meanings. The first meaning is to adhere to one, devoted to one. We are devoted to God. The second meaning is being steadfastly attentive to; give unremitting care to a thing. We are attentive to God. The third is to continue all the time in a place. We are always continuing in the presence of God. The fourth is persevere and not to faint. We will not faint while going after God. The fifth is to show one's self courageous for. We show ourselves courageous for

God. The sixth is to be in constant readiness for one, to wait on one constantly. We are always waiting and ready for the return of Christ. This is what we should be. We should have all these qualities to be persevering for God in all the situations that we go through. This helps us to thrive because we are not falling into just going through life but facing life knowing that we are heading for God.

The third principle is to pray at all times. Psalm 122:6-8 says, "Pray for the peace of Jerusalem; may they prosper who love you. Peace be within your walls, prosperity within your palaces. For the sake of my brethren and companions, I will now say, "Peace be within you." We must be praying always but also be praying for the things that are on God's heart. Like Jerusalem. When we do this we are affecting things in the heavenly realm that will ultimately accomplish something in this world. Matthew 9:37-38 says, "Then He said to His disciples, "The harvest is truly plentiful, but the laborers are few. Therefore pray to the Lord of the harvest to send out laborers into His harvest." In this verse Jesus is saying how there are many that will come to Christ if given the chance. That is what the harvest is. The people that are to bring the message of Christ are the laborers and they are few. We are to pray that God would put on people's hearts the desire to go into the field and bring people all over the world to Christ. This makes an impact on the whole world.

Ephesians 6:18 also says to make supplication for all the saints. The Greek word for supplication is deesis which means a seeking, asking, entreating, and entreaty to God or man. We are to prayerfully ask God for Him to change the world, to send people into the harvest, to help us battle temptations and sin, and to guide us in every way of our life. That is supplication and all of this helps us to make and impact in the world so that we are not merely surviving but also thriving.

CHAPTER 13

Demons

Well we have finally made it to this chapter. I am sure that you have probably been cringing because you knew this chapter was going to come up. I get it. It is very scary to even think about demons, and yet I am going to do an entire chapter discussing them. The reason I want to do this is because it is a great part of Spiritual Warfare and we must know who we are battling against. Ephesians 6:12 says, "For we do not wrestle against flesh and blood, but against principalities, against powers, against the rulers of the darkness of this age, against spiritual hosts of wickedness in the heavenly places." This is what we are battling against and this is all demons. At the beginning I talked about our main enemy, which is the devil, but he most likely does not know who you are. He is just the leader and he has deployed demons to tempt you to sin. The only way that the devil will know about you is if you are causing a lot of problems for him in this war. That is why I do not only want to be known in heaven but also in the deepest pit of hell. I want to cause so many problems for the devil that he trembles when I wake up. My feet should hit the floor and the devil cringe at the idea that I am awake because I am going to change the world. This is what I want to be but it is also very scary because that means I will face a lot of opposition from demons and the devil. It is dangerous to live this way, but I know that God will be with me and I know where I get to go when I die. I hope that many of you reading this have that kind of passion in your hearts because we need more people that are ready to run out in battle and destroy the demons that are in this world. It will be extremely hard and terrifying but it is what we need to do to win this war.

First I do want to share some stories about demons so that you can be sure that there is demonic activity in this world. I do not want you to think that they are too powerful because of these stories though. They are just to make you aware of what demons have done in this world. As C. S. Lewis said, "There are two equal and opposite errors which our race can fall into about the devils. One is to disbelieve in their existence. The other is to believe and feel an excessive and unhealthy interest in them." We do not want to fall into either of these errors, so as I share some of these stories, know that they are just to show you the demonic activity in this world.

The first story I want to share is about a friend's family. My friend was a missionary kid who lived in Mexico. At one time another family came to her parents and wanted them to come and cast out the demons they had in their house. What was happening is the house was inhabited by many demons and at night dolls in their daughter's room would be possessed and they would actually move and talk. The entire family would be terrorized by the demons in their house. When my friend's parents went into their house, they had to spend a few hours in there and they prayed over every object in the house to cast out all the demons. Finally, all the demons left the house and the family who lived there was brought to Christ because they saw that my friend's family served a real God that defeated the devil and demons terrorizing them.

The second story is about a pastor. One night he suddenly felt a very heavy weight come on top of him in bed and it felt like someone was choking him because he could not breathe. He knew in order to cast out the demon, he needed to speak but could not breathe so he prayed in his head to Jesus to come and cast the demon out and it left. Then in the morning he went to take a shower and when he took off his shirt, his body was all black and blue. The demon attacked him and bruised his entire body and tried to kill him by choking him to death.

The next story is about a woman who was molested by her father when she was young. When her father left the room after molesting her she said that a friend would come in her room and comfort her. The Bible calls this a comforting spirit. Later in her life after she was free of her father, the spirit would come in and rape her as her father did. She went to her pastor and he prayed over her and she became free of the spirit through much prayer. Demons can and will disguise themselves as something good like a friend so that we do not defend ourselves against them and instead let them get to us.

The last story is actually about me. When I was fifteen I went on a mission trip to Zambia. While we were there we faced a lot of demonic oppression. One night all the guys met together to discuss how the trip was going and see what was happening with each other. We were walking near the edge of the campsite that we were staying at and we suddenly saw a circle of dark figures around our entire camp. We saw demon forces.

There is more to the story but I am not going to finish it now.

These are the four stories that best show how demonic activity can work in this world. Now I want to see how we defend ourselves from demons. The first point we must know is that demons are over certain areas. The word principality means the position or authority of a prince. Demons are given authority by the devil over certain areas on the globe. When you believe this, it can explain a lot about our world. For instance, you can stand on a border of two countries and in the country on your right people are free to follow Christ, in the country on your left it is illegal to be a Christian. This can only happen when there are different demons over certain areas. This also shows that in certain areas demons are being fought off more. The United States of America is still known as a nation with freedom of religion, but it might not be long before we lose that freedom and I believe it is because we do not have people fighting the demonic forces that are controlling our nation. This means that we need to pray for every country geographically. When we pray against demons we must pray that the demons over America will be overcome. We can even be as specific as the demons over Texas, but we need to say the exact name of the place we are praying for. We can just pray for demons all over the world to be overcome. But it is more effective to be specific in your prayers. Also study the nations you are praying over so that you can pray about the specific things happening in the nation because of demons. Also when praying against demons and the devil we must speak it out loud. Demons cannot read our minds, so we must speak to them to be cast out with the power of Jesus Christ. There is one problem that people can fall into about this though. The problem is that sometimes people talk more to the devil in their prayers than to God. Remember that prayer is first for you to connect with God and then to pray for everything else you want to see happen in this world. This is how we can be effective against demons in the world.

The second point is to know that demons have you as an assignment. Every demon is given an assignment and one of the assignments given to demons is to make a person stop following God. They usually do this through making us sin. In C. S. Lewis's book *The Screwtape Letters* a demon is mentoring another demon on how to make a human fall, which is what his assignment was. This is how demons work. They are supposed to make you fall. What happens is that they tempt you with certain things and when you fall into sin they will continue to tempt you with that sin because you have fallen to it before. After a while the demons could get you addicted to this sin and they can actually stop tempting you. They would stop because you begin to run to that sin on your own. This is the worst place to be because that is when it is the hardest to stop the sin. I have been in this place too and it is extremely hard to battle sin when this happens. The way we battle demons when they tempt us is to find what they are tempting you with and pray specifically to not fall into that certain sin. Find Scripture about it and quote the Scripture in your prayer. Then with the power of Christ, command the demons to leave. When the demons leave they cannot tempt you anymore but you can still tempt yourself if you have become an addict. If this happens, you need to renew your mind. One way to do this is to live the opposite of what you are tempted with. If you are tempted with pride then find ways to be humble or do things that are humbling. If you are tempted with lust then live pure with the opposite sex. Now do not put yourself in danger of being tempted, but find ways in life to live differently than your mind wants you to if you are still being tempted. That is the best way to combat the demons who are assigned to you.

The third and final point is that demons can only enter where a doorway has already been opened for them. Demons cannot open a door into where they want to go. If they want to possess a mind, the doorway to the mind must already be opened for them. We open doors for demons all the time without even knowing. You can never make sure that there is no doorway open for them but we can do things to keep certain doorways closed. I want to discuss some of the things that we do to open doorways to demons.

The first is movies. Most of the horror movies that are made are about demons. Movies like *Paranormal Activity* or *The Unborn* are about demons. These movies can open doorways for demons. When we watch movies like this it enters into our mind which opens a door for demons to come into your mind because you are thinking about them. I am not saying that anything that has a slight demonic theme to it is completely bad. You can still watch movies, but you must know to guard your mind to opening a doorway that demons may be able to come through. The number one movies that focus on demons are horror movies. So one suggestion I have is to not watch a lot of horror movies. I have seen some horror movies, and some of them are really good, but I believe that we should stay as far away from the ones about demons as we can.

The second are books. If you did not know it there are actually a lot of demonic themes in Harry Potter. The woman that wrote Harry Potter was part of the occult and she had many experiences with summoning demons. Because of this some of that was brought into her books. No matter what you are writing your beliefs will sometimes subconsciously affect it. This is what happened with Harry Potter. Some of her beliefs were entered into the books. Also all the spells used in the books are real spells that she used during certain occult ceremonies. By reading them you are letting those spells into your mind which can open a door to demons. I do know some Christians who have read all the Harry Potter books and they were fine, but it is still something that can open a door. One good way to stay away from this is to read from Christian authors. I am not saying you must read only Christian books, but there are many Christian authors that write good fictional stories. For example, Veronica Roth is a Christian and she is the one that wrote the Divergent series, which is a great series. They do not need to be super spiritual books, but just try to stay away from books that may have demonic themes.

The third are certain games. There is a card game called *The Magic Gathering.* I do not know much about it because I have never played it myself, but in the game you have cards that summon certain things to fight the other people's cards. There are also ways to perform curses and enchantments with these cards. The problem with this is that it lets into your mind the thoughts of summoning monsters and other evil things to fight for you. It also makes evil things to be considered good because they can help you win. Because of this it can open a doorway into your mind. It is a lot like summoning demons. Many people will reply to this saying that when they use it, it is just a game to them. Well it is the same as using a Ouija (wee gee) board. That is just a game, yet many demonic things happen when people use it. These are just some things that can open a door to demons and it is best to stay away from them.

There are other ways to open doors but these are the main ones and most of the other ones have to do with personal things. To find those out, it is best to pray to God and ask Him if things are opening a doorway to demons. By knowing all this we can be effective at battling demons and begin to push back the armies of the devil.

Before I leave this chapter, there is one thing I need to make clear. I have many friends that are great Christians who read *Harry Potter*, watch many horror movies, and even play games like *Magic the Gathering*. Even though they do this, they have not been attacked greatly by demons. You can choose to do all of these things, but I just want you to know what you are letting into your minds, and want you to be aware of what could happen.

CHAPTER 14

Angels

In the last chapter we looked at the servants of Satan and how demons work in this world. Now it is fitting to talk about the servants of God, which are angels. As I have said before, the spiritual world is always affecting the physical world. Demons are a part of the negative way that the spiritual world is affecting the physical world. Angels are a part of the positive way. One thing we should ask ourselves is how am I affecting the spiritual war? If we are engaging in Spiritual Warfare, then anything we do will affect the spiritual world. We will never be effective spiritual warriors if all we think about is the demons that are tempting and attacking us. To be an effective warrior we need to believe that there are angels in this room right now. Know that wherever you are, there are angels there with you. Hebrews

12:22 says, "But you have come to mount Zion and to the city of the living God, the heavenly Jerusalem, to an innumerable company of angels." This verse is talking about when the Israelites were in the wilderness being led by God and God talked to Moses on top of a mountain. All the Israelites were extremely afraid and God told them that He was there but they did not want to go up the mountain and meet with Him because of their fear. Instead they had only Moses go up. This was where they got the instructions of how to build the tabernacle which was the first time that God would be able to dwell with His people. This is also where the angels will dwell. Now that Christ has come, we can have God dwell in us which means that we also have angels over us.

Hebrews 1:14 says, "Are they not all ministering spirits sent forth to minister for those who will inherit salvation?" The spiritual world is also ministering to this world through angels. Psalm 91:11 says, "For He shall give His angels charge over you, to keep you in all your ways." Matthew 18:10 says, "Take heed that you do not despise one of these little ones, for I say to you that in heaven their angels always see the face of My Father who is in heaven." These two verses say that each person has an angel over them. It says that God has given angels charge over you and that the angels always see God's face. Just as there are demons assigned to us, there are also angels who are assigned to us. Because of this we must know the difference. Demons will not always tempt you but they can speak into your mind things that sound good that will make you stumble later. The way we know that it is a demon is that if anything it says contradicts the Word of God. Angels will always minister to you the truth of God's Word.

Angels move when we pray. God will always send angels to do what you ask Him to do in prayer. Angels are the servants of God so they do the work of God in the world. I want to share a story that shows that angels move in our prayers and that there is a specific angel over all of us. This story comes from Acts 12:1-17. King Herod had harassed some of the people in the church. He had killed James and then seized Peter and threw him in jail. The church was in constant prayer for God to release Peter. That night an angel sent by the Lord came to Peter's jail cell and woke Him up and the chains fell off of Peter. The angel then asked Peter to put on his sandals and garment and to follow him out of the jail. They passed by all the guard posts and the gate opened for them to be led out. This happened because the people of God had prayed to Him for Peter to be released. Peter went to the place where the church was praying for him and knocked on the door of the gate. A girl named Rhoda came to answer. When she realized it was Peter, she did not open the gate but ran back inside and announced to everyone that Peter was at the gate. All the people thought she was crazy because they thought Peter was in prison. They were praying for Peter to be released but truly did not believe that he could be released. They then assumed that it was Peter's angel. The early churches believed that everyone had a specific angel that would watch over them. When they let Peter inside, they were astonished that it was truly him.

Now I want to discuss the three primary things that angels do. I have discussed this earlier in the book so it is a little bit of review, but I do want to go over it. The first thing that angels do is fight. Michael is the archangel of warriors. An archangel is an angel that is given charge over a group of other angels. Michael is the one that went up against Satan in battle when he was cast out of heaven. Daniel 10:12-13 says, "Then he said to me, "Do not fear, Daniel, for from the first day that you set your heart to understand, and to humble yourself before your God, your words were heard; and I have come because of your words. But the prince of the kingdom of Persia withstood me twenty-one days; and behold, Michael, one of the chief princes, came to help me, for I have been left alone there with the kings of Persia." David had been praying for three weeks but the angel had not been able to come to him because he was stuck with the kings of Persia until Michael came to help him. Michael was sent in as a warrior to fight against what was controlling the king of Persia. This also shows that we should not give up on prayer. David continued to pray for three weeks to God and was finally answered even though it was heard from the first day he started praying. We can know that we are always heard when we pray even if what we want does not happen right then. We must still continue to pray for it because we will see it be answered. God will not let your needs go unanswered if what you are praying for is His will.

The second thing angels do is send messages. Gabriel is the archangel of messages. Luke 1:19 says, "And the angel answered and said to Him, "I am Gabriel, who stands in the presence of God, and I was sent to speak to you and bring you these glad tidings." Gabriel was sent to tell Zacharias that he was going to be the father of John the Baptist. Luke 2:9-11 says that an angel was sent to proclaim to the shepherds that Christ has been born.

The third thing that angels do is worship. Lucifer was the archangel of worship. He was to usher all the worship and direct the angels to worship God. Then in his heart he wanted to be worshiped and exalted like

God. He did not want to be above God but he wanted to be like God. Because of this he began to hold back some of the worship of God and then Michael and the armies of God went and battled against him and all his angels that were to also worship God. They were then all cast out of heaven and onto the earth so there was no one to worship God in heaven. That is why our most important duty in this world is to worship God. God has truly never fought the devil. The angels are the first ones to fight the devil, and now we are commanded to fight the devil.

To end this chapter I want to share with you my favorite story in the Bible about angels and then a story about angels that I have experienced. 2 Kings 6:15-17 says, "And when the servant of the man of God rose early and went out, there was an army, surrounding the city with horses and chariots. And his servant said to him, "Alas, my master! What shall we do?" So He answered, "Do not fear, for those who are with us are more than those who are with them." And Elisha prayed, and said, "Lord, I pray, open his eyes that he may see." Then the Lord opened the eyes of the young man, and he saw. And behold, the mountain was full of horses and chariots of fire all around Elisha." When we know and understand that God has angels protecting us and fighting for us we are able to always say, "There are more of us than there are of them." This gives us the security that we can win the war against the devil. The Lord opened up the man's eyes and he saw all the angels ready to fight for them and knew that they had nothing to worry about. We can walk out in this warfare knowing that we have nothing to worry about because we have angels surrounding us. Yes we will face opposition and have hardships, but in the end God will have his angels care for us until we are called home to heaven to be with God forever. Now I want to finish my story that I started in the last chapter. If you remember I was in Zambia on a mission trip and one night we were near the edge of our camp and we saw a circle of dark figures trying to get into our camp. What I did not tell you is that there was and army of angels also surrounding the camp that was fighting against them to keep them out. God sent his army to protect us so that we could minister to the people in Zambia and give them the salvation that Christ has offered to everyone in the world. Let us walk and fight in this war knowing that there are angels fighting along side of us every day.

CHAPTER 15

Our Future Hope

We have reached the end of our journey going through how to battle in Spiritual Warfare. I hope it has helped you much and that you are able to go forth and conquer everything that the devil will throw at you. Before we end though, I want to show you what will happen when Christ comes back and the devil is destroyed. What will happen after we fight this war? What will be the outcome of this warfare? What is our future hope?

After Jesus was resurrected He was called the first fruits. 1 Corinthians 15:20 says, "But now Christ is risen from the dead, and has become the first fruits of those who have fallen asleep." The first fruit means that He is the first installment of something to come. Now everything that Christ accomplished on the cross was great and it means everything, but it was just the first installment of something that is coming. He was the first installment of what is spoken of in Revelation 21:1-7. It says, "Now I saw a new heaven and a new earth, for the first heaven and first earth had passed away. Also there was no more sea. Then I, John, saw the holy city, New Jerusalem, coming down out of heaven from God, prepared as a bride adorned for her husband. And I heard a loud voice from heaven saying, "Behold, the tabernacle of God is with men, and He will dwell with them, and they shall be His people. God Himself will be with them and be their God. And God will wipe every tear from their eyes; there shall be no more death, nor sorrow, nor crying. There shall be no more pain, for the former things have passed away." Then He who sat on the throne said, "Behold, I make all things new." And He said to me, "Write, for these words are true and faithful." And He said to me, "It is done! I am Alpha and Omega, the Beginning and the End. I will give of the fountain of the water of life freely to Him who thirsts. He who overcomes shall inherit all things, and I will be his God and he shall be My son." Jesus was the first installment of new heaven and a new earth. The city of God is called New Jerusalem. A lot of people think of Revelation and just see it as a bunch of weird symbols and a lot of hard to understand things, and it does have some of that stuff in it, but we need to know who it was written to and why. Revelation was written by John who was the disciple that Jesus loved. He wrote it to seven churches that were facing a lot of terrible things. He wrote this to them to give them a living hope. When we understand Christ as the first installment of this and that we have a living hope, we are able to face things that we would normally not be able to face on our own. This enables us to go out in boldness and fight the Spiritual Warfare that is in this world.

The three points I want to look at about this hope is the nature of the hope, the need for this hope, and how you can receive it. First is the nature of this hope. The nature of this hope is that it is coming out of heaven onto the earth. This is hard for some people to grasp because we believe that in the end it will be a bunch of individual people being taken up to heaven. Actually the climax of everything is heaven coming down and transforming the earth. A lot of Christian thinking is influenced by Plato. Plato started a belief that said everything physical is bad and evil and that everything spiritual is holy and good. Because of this belief we have come to believe that Christ is going to redeem us from the physical. The truth is that Christ is going to redeem the physical. The spirit is not the only thing that is going to be redeemed but the body also. Jesus did not say that I am making all new things;

He said that I am making all things new. Heaven is going to come down and renew the earth. The nature of this hope is not just to sing in heaven all the time. That would be great and wonderful but it is more than that. If Jesus is the first fruit of this then it will be like when Jesus was resurrected. He walked on the earth. He talked and conversed with His disciples. He also ate fish with His disciples. There will be a great wedding feast on the earth. Also on this earth we have a great longing for relationship because our relationship with God was broken when Adam and Eve sinned. That relationship will be mended and we will be able to experience the world that we never had. The world will be fixed to the way it was at the beginning in the Garden of Eden. We will walk with God and talk with Him. We might even be able to marry like Adam and Eve. Everything will be turned back to how it was meant to be and we will be able to fulfill a lifestyle of worship. We will not be able to sin. We might remember what sin is but not be able to actually do it. Also I want you to think of the most beautiful thing that you have ever seen. Something that was just so amazing that you cannot describe it because no words truly give it justice. What you are thinking about right now is tainted by sin. In this renewed world it will be immeasurably more beautiful because there is no sin to taint it. This just makes me so excited to see what happens when Christ comes back because it will be amazing. This is all coming.

The second point is the need for this hope. For this we need to look at who John was writing to. These people were about to experience more death, more crying, and more mourning than anyone reading this book has ever, and probably ever will experience. At the end of the century, the Roman Emperor Domitian was the first emperor to do widespread persecution of the Christians. Christians had their homes taken away and plundered. Christians were sent into the arena to be torn into pieces by wild beasts. Christians were impaled on stakes and while still alive covered with pitch and lit on fire. Christians were also crucified by the hundreds along the road so that people coming in and out of Rome could see all the Christians hanging on crosses. Revelation was written to these people. John gave them this hope so that they would be able to face that. He gave them the new heaven and the new earth. He gave them a living hope. Because of this the Christians took their suffering with peace. They forgave the people that were persecuting them and even sang hymns as animals were coming at them to tear them to pieces. Because they did that, Christianity actually spread and the more Christians that were killed the more people became

Christians. This is because people saw that they had something real. They saw that they had something worth dying for and a true hope. It is a known fact that more people become Christians because of martyrs after the martyrs have died than before. That is because Christ is worth dying for. We do not need to fear death because we have a hope that is alive. One thing to know is that people are hope-shaped creatures. Basically the way that we live today is controlled by what we believe about our future. An example is that you put two men in a room and tell them every day they must perfectly screw a nail into a circle on the wall. And they must do as many of them as they can every day for a year. Then tell one of them that at the end of the year they will be given twenty thousand dollars. You tell the other one that at the end of the year you will give one of them twenty million dollars. Soon the one promised with twenty thousand dollars will give up and say that it is too tedious and awful. The man promised twenty million dollars will think this isn't tedious at all. He decides to continue because the outcome of going through this every day is so great. That is the way these Christians were. They went through it all because the outcome was going to be so great. If we cannot take the resurrection and new heaven and new earth seriously, then it is not a hope. We must know that all the evil and persecution and suffering on this earth is a passing thing. That is why John wrote that there would be no more death, nor sorrow, nor crying. All this is a passing thing and it will be replaced by a renewed earth. We need this so we can face everything that will ever come against us. When we truly engage in Spiritual Warfare there will be hard things that will come against us and we will need a reason to keep on going. The reason to keep on is the same hope that gave thousands of Christians the ability to persevere through the worst deaths ever experienced.

The last point is how we receive this hope. We receive this by believing in the death and resurrection of Jesus Christ. There is no other way. If you want this hope, then you must grasp and understand and believe in the cross. On the cross Christ experienced the cosmic thirst that we deserve so we could have a hope that cannot be crushed. Jesus Christ experienced hopelessness because God actually separated Himself from His Son and Jesus died. Jesus Christ lost everything He had. He experienced the hopelessness that we deserve. That is what He did for us. Then there was also the resurrection. He rose and is seated on a throne and declares that He is making everything new. Jesus is the beginning of the newness of life. He is the first fruit and eventually everything will be made new.

Death hit Jesus and now the only thing that can hit us is the shadow of death and it is our entrance into glory. That is why we wage this war. It is because of the hope that Jesus Christ has given us. We are not scared of death or of anything that the devil tries to throw at us because we have the living hope that John wrote about to the Christians facing persecution at that time. I want to end this book with a passage of Scripture that talks about Jesus being the first fruits and how creation groans for the redemption that will be brought when Jesus returns. I want you to see this scripture with the thought of the earth being renewed in mind and know that this is the hope that we are looking forward to. The passage is Romans 8:18-25. It says, "For I consider that the sufferings of this present time are not worthy to be compared to the glory that will be revealed in us. For the earnest expectation of the creation eagerly waits for the revealing of the sons of God. For creation was subjected to futility, not willingly, but because of Him who subjected it in hope; because the creation itself will also be delivered from the bondage of corruption into the glorious liberty of the children of God. For we know that the whole creation groans and labors with birth pangs together until now. Not only that, but we also who have the first fruits of the Spirit, even we ourselves groan within ourselves, eagerly waiting for the adoption, the redemption of our body. For we were saved in this hope, but hope that is seen is not hope; for why does one still hope for what he sees? But if we hope for what we do not see, we eagerly wait for it with perseverance."

Quotes and Information

Dean Sherman

Sun Tzu

Tony Herring

Kent Hovind

Randy Templeton

Mark Driscoll

Adolf Hitler

Smith Wigglesworth

Switchfoot

C.S. Lewis

Plato

Timothy Keller

Verses: